MG MIDGET
AUSTIN-HEALEY SPRITE
(EXCEPT 'FROGEYE')

Lindsay Porter

CONTENTS

Foulis

Haynes

Further titles in this series will be published at
regular intervals. For information on new titles
please contact your bookseller or write to the
publisher.

ISBN 0 85429 344 2

A FOULIS Motoring Book

First published 1983

© **Haynes Publishing Group**

Published by:
Haynes Publishing Group
Sparkford, Yeovil,
Somerset BA22 7JJ

Distributed in USA by:
Haynes Publications Inc.
861 Lawrence Drive, Newbury
Park, California 91320, USA

Editor: Rod Grainger
Cover design: Rowland Smith
Page Layout: Gill Carroll
Cover picture: Steve Coley's
Midget & Martin Francis' Sprite
photographed by Lindsay Porter
Printed in England by: J.H.Haynes &
Co. Ltd

FOREWORD

The M.G. Midget, née Austin-Healey Sprite, ceased production in November 1979 and in that sense could now be thought of as a car of the past. In many other ways, however, the Sprites and Midgets are very much sports cars for today!

Frugal in their use of petrol, easy to service, maintain and even rebuild, and with a reputation for reliability that is second to none, the Sprites and Midgets possess attributes that many manufacturers would give their eye teeth to be able to proclaim in their current sales pitch. Obviously, there *are* defects and deficiencies, which is hardly surprising in a car whose basic design goes back to the fifties. But in spite of the criticisms, the 'Spridgets' (as they are often nicknamed) possess one attribute that is valuable today perhaps more than ever; they are the epitome of pure, unadulterated, motoring fun!

To be a Spridget enthusiast is to appreciate the delights of touch-sensitive steering allied to road holding that leaves most of its competitors looking foolish. No fixed-head version ever came off the production lines and so every Spridget owner knows the incomparable feeling of freedom and of one-ness with the surroundings to be experienced in a car with the top removed. He or she even learns to live with the feelings of one-ness with every bump in the road!

After an eighteen year production span (or twenty-one if the earlier 'Frogeye' Sprite is included), enthusiasts on both sides of the Atlantic are still spoiled for choice if they want one of these delightful little cars. After all, over 300,000 were built. From the crudely simple early cars with quarter-elliptic rear springing and a complete lack of refinement through to the soft-nosed, softly appointed 1500 with Triumph engine, the enthusiast can take his or her pick. One thing is certain, he/she won't end up with a characterless clone car produced by the robots of our brave new world but a car which, though modest and unassuming in many ways, has a zest for living which leaves the others standing!

The reader will find that this *Super Profile* is an affectionate but objective cameo of the Sprites from Mk II onwards and the Midgets from 1961, in all their different guises, through to the car's final demise. Although only a small publication, between these covers will be found a highly detailed and well rounded picture of one of the most fun-to-own sports cars of all time.

I would like to take this opportunity to thank all of those people who helped so wholeheartedly in the production of this book, all the owners who kindly allowed me to photograph their cars at the Avoncroft Museum of Buildings, Bromsgrove, near Birmingham and other venues and especially my friends Grahame Sykes and Jed Watts at Spridgebits who gave many hours of their time to identifying elusive production change points and provided a great deal of practical advice and technical information, as always in their quietly dependable and extremely thorough way. Lastly, *Motor* and *Autocar* magazines kindly allowed us to reproduce their contemporary road tests of the various Sprites and Midgets – a very valuable addition to this publication.

Lindsay Porter

HISTORY

Family Tree

The late 1950s and early 1960s were exciting times for much of the British motor industry. It was a time of expansion, of change, even in some ways, of revolution. The Mini had made its debut in 1959 causing little immediate splash but creating ripples which were to grow and grow with the passing of time. The E-type Jaguar of 1961 was a production car of phenomenal power and no little comfort of a type which has since been sadly missed. It was in this atmosphere of confidence that BMC felt able to introduce the Austin-Healey Sprite, a sports car which the mass market could afford for the first time, after years of postwar austerity. As British Prime Minister, Harold Macmillan was to say to the British people at the time "You've never had it so good!" He might just as easily have been directing his comments towards the British motorist.

The original Austin-Healey Sprite with its 'frog-eye' headlamps had first seen the light of day in May 1958. The original design lasted for three years before BMC introduced a rebodied version of the car. At that time short production spans were becoming the norm rather than the exception;

tooling and development costs were lower than they are today and could be more easily recouped. BMC must, even in 1961, have envisaged a time when the car would once again require complete revision. They would no doubt have been amazed to the point of disbelief if it had been suggested that the basic package would last not three but *eighteen* years before it was phased out. But that is exactly what did happen as this remarkable Peter Pan of a car continued to be produced so successfully while never seeming to grow any older.

To know where to begin to look at the history and evolution of this fine little car, it helps to catch a glimpse of the form it took at the conclusion of its production life. The MG Midget 1500, announced in 1975 (the Sprite option had by then been discontinued), was fitted with a Triumph engine in place of the Austin A-series unit which had seen service in the car since its inception (albeit in steadily increasing sizes), while the body was virtually unchanged since the days of 1961. Right up to the time of its demise, the sill line maintained its strange kick-up at the front; strange, that is, only until it is realised that the shape of the sill was determined by the shape of the *original* 1958 Sprite's fold-forward bonnet.

The original Sprite had been designed almost entirely by the Healey Motor Company at Warwick while many of the 1961 modifications and production from first to last had been carried out by M.G. at Abingdon. So it can be seen that the car became a highly successful amalgam of components and ideas from Healey, Austin, M.G. and Triumph plus a significant contribution from Morris. The possibility of this cross-fertilisation came about because of the peculiar relationships which have existed within the British motor industry over the last few decades.

The M.G. concern was formed by William Morris when, in the

1920s 'The Morris Garages' began to build their own Morris-based sports cars. Much later, in 1952, the two giants of the British motoring scene, Austin and Morris, amalgamated, with Austin's Chairman Len Lord becoming Chairman of the newly formed British Motor Corporation. In the same year Lord approached Geoffrey Healey and struck a liaison which led to the production of the first Austin-Healey sports car. Meanwhile, Triumph, another great name of pre-Second World War days, had been making its own connections and became part of a group which included Standard, Alvis, Rover and the Leyland truck and bus concern. In 1968, both large groups were locked together in a giant organisation called British Leyland within which, at least in the world of saloon and sports cars, the old Triumph management were top dogs.

Of all these famous names, the most important in this story are those of Healey, Austin and M.G.. Although M.G. were scarcely involved at all in the design of the original Sprite but only became concerned when the car was first revised, in some ways their history is the most influential because they, more than any other marque, paved the way for the concept of the light British sports car, a tradition taken on by the Sprite. In 1923, the M.G. Car Company began rebodying 'Bullnose' Morris Oxfords and by 1928, the first sports cars were being produced. One was a large and prestigious six-cylinder car known as the 18/80, while the other, the M-type Midget, based on the overhead camshaft Morris Minor of the day, was the real sales success. Its successor, the J-type midget, set the trend for all light sports cars produced by M.G. up to 1955, when the emphasis switched to a slightly larger format with the introduction of the MGA. Thus, the original 'Frogeye' Sprite and its successors were simply filling a void left by the demise of the small M.G. and taking over both its traditions and its established export markets.

This marketing void had been spotted by Austin's Leonard Lord who called Donald Healey, head of the Healey Motor Company, to a meeting to discuss the possibility of a new light sports car. Since 1952, the two concerns had worked together with great success following Austin's adoption of the Healey 100 which was then renamed as an Austin-Healey. Even before their design for the aggressively attractive Healey 100, Geoffrey Healey had already made a considerable name for himself on both sides of the Atlantic for his range of sporting saloons and open cars, the most famous of which was the competition-bred Healey Silverstone. The Warwick-based concern had always been something of a shoe-string affair, unable to break out of the vicious circle caused by not having sufficient funds to boost production enough to be able to benefit from economies of scale and so not having large enough production to create sufficient funds. As a result, bought-in Riley power and drive trains had to be used until production of the Riley units ceased. At that point, Healey collaborated with the Nash Kelvinator Corporation of the U.S.A. out of which came the Nash-Healey, some welcome funds for the Healey company and a chance for Donald Healey to cut his teeth in dealings with a much larger and more powerful partner.

Although Healey designed and built the prototype Sprites, the whole car with the exception of Morris steering rack and rear brakes and an M.G. brake/clutch master cylinder, was based on Austin mechanical components. They had all come from the Austin A35, successor to the 1951 A30 (itself designed as a postwar version of the famous Austin Seven), of which 290,000 had been produced. The Austin Seven had been so popular, versatile and durable that a very large number of

variants were produced. Among them were the sporting Ulster and Nippy – Austin's only small sports cars before the Sprite. Quite a number of Seven sports cars were raced, providing an enjoyable and low cost introduction to sports car racing for many people. The 1951 Austin A30 engine was quickly pressed into use in the existing Morris Minor after the amalgamation of the two manufacturers. The Minor, however, was a heavier car than the A30 and the engine, still only of 802cc capacity, was not capable of propelling the car's three-quarters of a ton at anything like a respectable speed. In 1956, the engine was bored out to 948cc and the bores siamesed to accommodate the extra capacity. The engine was redesigned in many ways and became a somewhat more lively unit with a delightfully smooth and willing feel to it. It also had great reserves of strength which was significant in view of the tuning which was to come in the future. The Austin gearbox was also installed in the Minor as well as the rear axle to keep it company. In 1956, in conjunction with the engine modifications, the gearbox was given a remote gearchange to replace the long, sloppy, 'pudding-stirrer' previously fitted.

At much the same time, the Standard Motor Company were busily introducing their own small car, the Standard Eight, with styling remarkably similar to that of the A30. Its engine, too, was of an identical size and it was also to be modified and enlarged before long. In 1954, the Standard Ten was offered as an option, this time fitted with a 948cc version of the original engine, the same size, amazing coincidence though it may seem, as BMC's 1956 engine enlargement. After Standard was taken over by Triumph, the engine was used in a new Triumph saloon car, the Herald, in 1959 and later in the Spitfire sports car in 1962, although by then the engine had been expanded to 1147cc. In

1967, the Standard engine was enlarged to 1296cc and then again to 1493cc for the front-wheel-drive Triumph 1500 in 1970. In 1974 the 1500cc engine was chosen to be fitted both to the Spitfire and to the Midget.

So it came to pass that the M.G. Midget of 1979, the last of the line, successor to the Austin-Healey Sprites and M.G. Midgets built from 1961 to 1971 and to the Austin-Healey Sprite MkI from 1958 to 1971, became a car descended from many sources. In spite of all that, Geoffrey Healey wrote in 1978. 'I drove one [of the last Midgets] recently. It was still a Sprite, with direct, responsive steering and safe handling, and I immediately felt at home in it'.

Concept

Two descriptions remain of how the concept behind the original 'Frogeye' Sprite was first expressed. Geoffrey Healey in his book, *More Healeys,* tells the tale of Austin's chief, Len Lord, meeting Donald Healey and discussing the then current state of the sports car market. "In his blunt, down to earth manner, Len Lord then commented that what we needed was a small, low cost sports car to fill the gap left by the disappearance of the Austin Seven Nippy and Ulster models of prewar fame. What he would really like to see, he said, was a bug. It is impossible to tell whether he was simply thinking aloud, or deliberately giving DMH [Donald Healey] a broad hint of what we should do ..."

Then, in 1977, Gerry Coker, once Healey's body designer wrote a letter of reminiscences to the Austin-Healey Owners' Club in which he said, "For 1956 Mr Healey wanted a cheap two-seater, 'that a chap could keep in his bike shed'."

The 'bug' that was simple and small enough to be afforded and owned by the sort of chap that owned a bicycle shed, came into being as the fairly spartan Mk I Sprite with no frills whatever, not even exterior door handles nor a boot. The Sprite Mk II/Midget Mk I that succeeded it maintained the tradition of function with fun but bowed to the inevitable pressures to modernise. Its steering was still the same and the thrills of attaining standards or road holding which were superior to almost everything else on four wheels were still there. In fact, in all essential respects the Sprites and Midgets were never to lose the sense of fun possessed by the very first cars. Only the details of the cars' construction changed, such as the wind-up windows which were fitted quite early on, and the wall to wall carpets which helped to keep the noise down in what was an inherently noisy car. Even though the engine size was increased at regular intervals through the car's life (no less than four different engine sizes, with a further major engine substitution thrown in for good measure, were used) this did not affect the car's character. It had never been a fast car and even with a 1500cc engine, it was still not especially quick. Of course it was faster than the original car had been but compared to the rest of the traffic on the road, the Sprite was still capable of being embarrassed by an even half decently quick saloon car ... that is, until the corners were reached!

Design and Evolution

Healeys were not the first to have toyed with the idea of a lightweight, low-cost sports car. Abingdon had already taken an MGA and fitted it out with an Austin A35 engine, only to find that the weight of the MGA body made the car impossibly slow. In the early fifties, Austin themselves had come up with a lightweight sporting car with a tubular space frame whose body style was reminiscent of the Jensen-built Austin A40 Sports.

Neither of these projects had come to anything and part of the reason was because a new, small sports car had to be especially light for its performance to be acceptable, and that meant building a car without a chassis. The Austin Healey Sprite was the first sports car to be constructed without a separate chassis. Instead, all the various loadings were fed into the main body structure.

To give this structure all of the rigidity it needed, the car's floorpan was made to do most of the work of a conventional chassis. The floor itself, the two box-section sills and the transmission tunnel were the major contributors to front-to-back stiffness while a pair of extra box-sections, welded to the top of the floor, one beneath each seat also ran front-to-back and helped carry the weight of the luggage compartment, spare wheel and fuel tank forwards into the main structure. At the rear of this central structure, just ahead of the rear wheels, was another box-section, this time of triangular section, into which the rear quarter-elliptic springs were fitted. The front of the body structure, the bulkhead area, was rather more complex but comprised, basically, a pair of boxes surrounding the occupants' legs and a vertical wall linking the two boxes together. At the top of this scuttle area, the steel dashboard provided extra lateral stiffening. Projecting forwards from the scuttle were a pair of more traditional-looking chassis legs to which the engine mountings were fitted and against which the front of the bonnet was held shut with catches. At the rear, there was no boot (trunk) lid for the simple reason that the rear panel was considered to be a 'stressed' area; that is, it contributed to the strength at the rear of the car and to have cut into it to provide a boot lid would have reduced that strength as well as incurring a weight penalty.

The rear suspension was, if anything, even more revolutionary

in concept, for an inexpensive car, than the unitary platform supporting it. Following the lead of the MkI Jaguar which was already in production at that time, the Sprite had quarter-elliptic rear springs. Unlike the more conventional half-elliptic springs which are located on the chassis at each end, quarter-elliptics are rigidly held by the bodyframe at one end and the axle is mounted at the other. The enormous amount of force which this placed upon the bodywork was absorbed in the Sprite by locating the springs in boxes let into the hollow rear panel. Further reinforcement was provided by a thick plate running under the floor while on the top of the floor extra strengthening was provided by a spot-welded channel section running in line with the springs. This type of system has the drawback that, under torque strains imparted from the car's drive, the axle is prone to fore and aft movement. Healey partially overcame this problem by placing radius arms directly above the springs and located at the top of the axle and the car's bodyframe. Even so, 'twitchiness' was always found to be a problem to some extent until, in October 1962, the MkIII Sprite/MkII Midget was introduced with half-elliptic springing. This was a relatively simple modification to make (compared with the Sprite redesign which led to the MkII, which was said to have cost more than the original design for the complete car!) because pick-up points for the rear of the new springs were easily attached to existing 'chassis' rails which swept over the rear axle line and through the boot. In fact, this alteration was so easily accomplished that one wonders whether the original Sprite body might not have been designed with the option of conventional rear suspension in mind?

At the front of the car, suspension loadings were taken primarily by the front 'chassis' legs which were tied together by a supporting crossmember. In common with the rest of the car's mechanical components, the front suspension itself came from the Austin A35 and on each side consisted of a single, pressed steel lower wishbone, a coil spring and an upper 'wishbone' formed by the Armstrong shock absorber lever arms. The brakes, too, were A35 units at the front but at the back they were Morris Minor components. The A35's rear brakes incorporated a mechanical handbrake linkage which was deemed unsuitable (not because it hung too low as some have sugggested: being mounted on the axle it would have hung no lower than on the saloon!) and the Minor's rear handbrake operating through the wheel cylinders was retained. It had been found at the design stage that the A35's steering system was too bulky to fit and so the Minor's rack and pinion system was chosen. Giving 2.5 turns from lock-to-lock, the rack gave delightfully positive steering when fitted to the Minor. To the Sprite, with its shorter wheel base, it gave steering as precise as anyone could ever wish for.

Changes made to the running gear over the years were relatively few in number. The front suspension remained basically unchanged apart from a little strengthening here and a little uprating there, as heavier engines were introduced but the front brakes were changed to discs fairly early on and the rear brakes were changed to the Mini type with separate handbrake mechanisms. Happily, the steering was never changed, allowing the Sprite to retain its inimitable character throughout its production life.

It was to the body and to the engine that most of the significant changes were made for later Sprites and Midgets. First, the body. The MkI Sprite body had been designed by the Healey concern at Warwick while Austin and M.G. made modifications where they would assist in the

actual mass-production of the cars. The MkII Sprite/MkI Midget was designed partly by Healey and partly by M.G., the front and rear halves being split between them, as already described. The M.G. contribution included sculpting out the rear cockpit area to make it larger, fitting a bootlid and squaring-up the look of the rear end, making it close in appearance to the rear end of the MGB which was then still to be announced. Healey's contribution was the more significant, however. The original one-piece front end was dispensed with, and orthodox wings with headlamps in the usual place were fitted. Some experiments were carried out using the original style of grille but in the end a wider grille with vertical slats was chosen for the M.G. Midget and a mesh styling was selected for the Sprite. There were very few other differences between the two cars except for some extra chrome and extra cost for the Midget version.

A Healey proposal to market a genuinely cheaper Sprite with rounded rear end and a spare wheel stowed away in a slot in the tail, in the manner of some of Healey's much earlier cars, was considered but finally rejected by the management. Rounded rear wheelarches *did* return to the cars in later years but were not to last long, being phased out because of the demands of American safety regulations (the cut-away wheelarch style reduced rear end

strength in the event of a rear end collision and the deeper, more squared-off wheel arches had to be reinstated). The only other body change worthy of note was the fitting of heavy, urethane covered bumpers, again at the demand of U.S. safety legislation. These were accompanied by an increase in ride height which did nothing for the car's handling although the extra weight of the bumpers is felt by some to have a beneficial inertia-damping effect and so to increase ride comfort.

In its A35 form, the engine was much too low powered even for a small sports car like the MkI Sprite. Consequently, it was lightly tuned by Eddie Maher at the Morris Engines Department and was fitted with twin $1\frac{1}{8}$ inch S.U. carburettors; valves and valve springs were strengthened as was the crank. For the MkII Sprite/Mk I Midget, basically the same engine was used but with more of the modifications that one would expect to see fitted to a sports car. HS2 ($1\frac{1}{4}$ inch) S.U. carburettors were fitted, as were a modified manifold, improved camshaft, larger inlet valves and higher compression pistons. The gearbox was still of the cone synchromesh type but its ratios were the same as the optional high ratio box previously offered to MkI owners.

Later engines were progressively modified and enlarged and gearboxes were drastically improved, although synchromesh on first gear was very late in arriving. The final engine change came about when B.L. had to modify engines quite considerably to meet increasingly stringent emission control standards from America. The solution they chose was to fit and modify a larger 1500cc engine to both the Midget and the Triumph Spitfire. The new engine gave a small but useful increase in bhp but a larger increase in available torque, allying more sports car 'punch' to the traditional Midget virtues.

Of the other alterations made to the car over the years — and there were many too small to be considered for inclusion here — the most significant include those to the interior. Although always stark by many people's standards, the interior of the Sprites and later the Midgets by themselves, changed out of all recognition when compared with the original car. They became far more comfortable, reclining seats were fitted along with a fold-down hood which was one of the very best of its type.

In eighteen years, the car had evolved from being a 'Frogeye' Sprite with a new style of body construction to a far more comfortable, more powerful sports car which had lost few, if any, of the original virtues while gaining a great deal in the way of 'usability' *en route*. Throughout the whole of its production life, which totalled twenty-one years if the earliest Sprites are included with the last Midgets, the car's basic 'rolling chassis' remained unchanged in all essentials, save that of the type of rear springs and front brakes used. The floorpan was never changed from that which John Thompson Motor Pressings had built for Donald Healey in the mid-fifties in prototype form, and even an echo of the original Sprite's one-piece bonnet was to be seen to the last in the shape of those upswept sills.

Variants

Just as the management had become anxious about the styling of the original Sprite and had rushed in a new design — unnecessarily in many people's opinion — they understandably seemed to be neurotic on occasions about the later Sprites and Midgets which were to become one of their resident Peter Pans of the production line. As a result, a number of replacement studies were made and a number of prototypes built, most of them based around the idea of Mini-style hydrolastic suspension and transversely mounted, front-wheel-drive engine. Both the Sprite/Midget engine and that of the MGB had been transposed into this mode for use in the Mini, the 1100 and the 1800, which must have seemed a logical step at the time, despite Alec Issigonis' known antagonism towards this type of layout being used in a space-wasting two-seater. Indeed the almost Svengali-like thrall in which he held those at Longbridge may have had something to do with the fact that neither the ideas put forward by Abingdon nor those by Longbridge were ever put into effect.

Another proposed change which was never put into production because of political rather than practical problems was a proposal to uprate the performance of the 1275cc engine by a considerable amount. Eddie Maher, the man who worked on the old A35 engine before it was fitted to the first Sprite, developed an engine which was marginally a better performer than the Mini-Cooper 'S' 1275 engine but which cost less to produce. Why was it never produced? Simply because it would have made the performance of the Sprites and Midgets uncomfortably close to that of the more expensive, larger-engined MGBs!

In reality, no major variations on the basic Sprite/Midget theme were ever to be produced, although one particular racing Sprite was considered to be a 'production' car for the purposes of the nudge-and-a-wink rules that attempt to govern international motor sport. The 'Sebring' Sprite was produced by the Healey concern at Warwick and was, in effect, a complete package of all the tuning equipment then available for the car. Although still based on the normal Sprite it was built in sufficient numbers for the car to be recognised and homologated as a separate car, a 'Grand Tourer', by the international authorities. Various stages of tune were available but the full house version was really some performer!

Other manufacturers have since capitalised upon the Sprite's involvement in motor sport by imitating the often spectacular looking bodywork used in this field. Because of the original car's structure, this is relatively simple to fit, especially where modifications are carried out to the front end; removal of existing front wings and the substitution of a GRP nose does little to reduce the car's strength. One firm which has been highly successful in the production of GRP replacement bodywork is the Lenham Motor Company which, following the 1964 Le Mans Race produced a Camm-tailed replica of the Le Mans Sprite. Fibreglass rear ends are still available today from Lenham and are fitted after cutting away most of the car's rear superstructure. At the front, the Lenham Superfast bonnet complements the appearance of the car.

An even more dramatically executed variation on the standard Sprite and Midget theme is that offered by Arkley. They offer GRP body panels that change the appearance of the car completely while retaining the use of the existing scuttle, floorpan, screen and doors. After conversion, the car looks like a cross between a beach buggy and a pre-war M.G.

Competition

Competition is almost invariably in the blood of the men who make motor cars. Yet at B.M.C. the approach was somewhat ambivalent. The official line for many years was that there was little money to be 'squandered' on the vaingloriousness of racing but somehow, Sprites and Midgets were always raced; at least up until 1968 with less than hidden factory co-operation.

With Sprites, the deception

was relatively simple. Funds were diverted to Warwick where the Healey concern prepared and fully involved themselves with race-going cars. Abingdon's involvement was rather more undercover but it was certainly there, nonetheless. Early in 1962, they signalled the start of real Midget-based racing operations by building three attractive looking and rather successful fixed-head coupes which were often to race alongside the mainly open cars from Warwick.

Of course, Sprites and Midgets must have taken part in hundreds of races over the years. They are so easy to buy, tune and maintain that they have always been the ideal 'clubman's' car. Inevitably, the reverse side of this coin is that they have never been terribly competitive – at least not to the extent of achieving overall wins. What follows here is a selection culled from the many class successes (and a tiny handful of overall victories) achieved by the cars when they were in their heyday and when they were factory prepared.

1962
Class win in Monte Carlo Rally for Sprite driven by Riley and Hughes, 3rd, 6th, 7th and 9th at Sebring. Drivers included Moss, Rodriguez, Ireland and one Steve McQueen.

1963
Sprite gained Class Win at Monte Carlo driven by Riley and Hughes. First and Third in Class for Midget special bodied coupes in *Autosport* Championship.
Sprite coupe gained First in Class in Sebring 12-Hour race.

1964
First and Second in Class for Midgets in Nurburgring 500-mile race (they were also the highest placed British cars).
At Sebring, a Sprite won its Class driven by Baker and Colgate.

1965
Sebring saw 1293cc Sprites come 15th and 18th while a Midget

coupe finished 26th overall, First in its class.
At the Targa Florio, Sprite number TFR 2 (Aaltonen and Baker) came 15th overall, 2nd in Class, while the Hopkirk/Hedges Midget coupe finished 11th overall and also 2nd in its Class.
At the West-Coast venue of Bridgehampton, Aaltonen came First in Class and Makinen Third in a Midget coupe.
A Midget coupe finished First overall in the Kingsway Trophy Race at Phoenix Park, Dublin, driven by Alec Poole.
Le Mans saw a Sprite finish a creditable 12th overall, First in Class.

1966
At Sebring, 'Le Mans' Sprites finished First and Second in Class. 3rd in Class (16th overall) achieved by Sprite coupe (TFR 4) driven by Aaltonen and Baker at the Targa Florio.
First in Class for a Midget at the Brands Hatch 500-Mile race.

1967
Sebring: Sprites First and Second in Class, although winner actually a Midget MII rebodied as a Mk I Sprite!
At Le Mans, Hedges and Baker averaged 100mph for the first time in a Sprite. 15th overall and *Motor* Trophy for best placed British car. Roger Enever's 1293cc fuel-injected car and John Britten's 1148cc 8000rpm-engined metamorphosed Midget (ie, converted Sprite) held, between them, Class records at Silverstone, Brands, Mallory and six other circuits. Britten won the Amasco Championship based on the number of events won in the year.

1968
Healey re-labelled a Sprite as a Midget (for publicity purposes) and won the Sports Car Category outright at Sebring, 15th overall (ahead of a GT40!) Fuel-injected Sprite First in Prototype Class. Sprite number TFR 6 with 1293cc

dry sump engine won Class in Mugello, Florence.
15th overall at Le Mans.

M.G.'s and Healey's race programmes were subsequently halted upon the formation of British Motor Holdings (later British Leyland). Abingdon Competitions Department turned its attention to Triumphs and other B.L. makes until, in August 1970, the Department was abruptly closed down. 'Privateers' continued to campaign their cars, notably the Ring Free Oil Racing Team which achieved 1st and 2nd in Class at Sebring in 1969.

Success Reviewed

Taken as a whole, the production of the Sprites and Midgets was remarkably consistent. During its three main years of production, the 'Frogeye' Sprite sold 48,999 units, an average of just over 16,000 per year. From 1961 on, when the car was rebodied and sold as the car(s) covered here, the combined sales of Sprites and Midgets totalled 306,899 – again an average of just over 16,000 per year.

The 'Spridget's' amazing consistency of sales (except for the very end, but more of that in a while) reflects no more than the unchanging appeal of the basic model. For a sports car, it has always been a safe car to own; sporting in its feel and response on the road, fun to drive with the top down, but always predictable in its road behaviour and always leaving the driver feeling fully in control. Of course, the cars were modified and given the 'de luxe' treatment but these changes were always brought about in response to the motoring norms of the day. Even so, such an ancient structure was bound to be feeling its age after twenty-one years of production. In comparison with a sit-up-and-beg Ford Popular, the original 'Frogeye' must have felt almost comfortable as well as incredibly quick. By the side of a Ford Fiesta, it was the Midget 1500 which seemed to be the motoring throwback.

To the planners, the model's end must have seemed inevitable. Speak to any of them today and they will tell a tale of falling sales, of unsold stocks and of cutbacks in production. Indeed, in 1979, the total production was only 9,777 cars, the first time the figure had ever dropped below five figures. (Production finished in November of that year, incidentally, leaving only eleven production months available).

What the planners fail to point out is that they had created a self-fulfilling prophecy and brought about the demise of the cars themselves. They did so by manipulating price levels until the cars were no longer affordable by the ordinary man or woman who would otherwise have bought the car. The effects of inflation disguise what really happened, but if those effects are stripped away the results are interesting. The new selling price of the M.G. Midget in June 1961 was £682 (and remember that the Sprite was around twenty pounds cheaper). By September 1974, the price had risen to £1204 but, after allowing for inflation, the actual cost was only 83% of the original price. The price had fallen! By November 1979, the cost was up to £3821 which represented no less than 128% of the car's original price *after* the effects of inflation have been taken into account. The car had changed from being a low priced car, likely to appeal to a large number of people, to being both out of date *and* overpriced. No wonder it failed!

EVOLUTION

**May 1961 A-H Sprite MkII.
Chassis numbers H-AN6 101 to
H-AN6 24731.**
More powerful 948cc engine now
giving 52bhp (SAE) from modified
camshaft, larger valves, different
(higher compression ratio) pistons,
SU HS2 ($1\frac{1}{4}$ inch) carbs replacing
earlier $1\frac{1}{8}$ inch type. HS2
carburettors now with plastic
dashpot top screws in place of
earlier brass type and with modified
choke linkage. Different inlet and
exhaust manifolds now fitted, the
exhaust manifold being one piece in
place of the earlier type with top
blanking plate.

Gearbox still with smooth
casing (later types have a ribbed
casing) but with higher ratio gears
identical to those in the optional
high ratio gearbox offered to MkI
Sprite owners.

Trim identical to Frogeye
Sprite except for changes of switch
position, lever switches fitted in
place of push-pull type, barrel type
lighting switch (surrounding
ignition switch) replaced by flick
switch, and relative position of
headlamp and ignition warning
lights, mounted in tachometer and
speedometer dials, reversed.

Extensive bodywork changes
as described in text and hood and
tonneau modified to suit new rear
bodywork. Single piece hood frame
replaced by split type and storage
bag provided.

**June 1961. M.G. Midget MkI.
Chassis numbers G-AN1 101 to
G-AN1 16183.**
Similar to Sprite in most respects
although price was £20 higher plus
Purchase Tax in the U.K.. Detail
changes to justify price increment
and change of marque name: waist
rail chrome strips on bodywork,
centre chrome finishing strip on
bonnet, plain chrome hub caps
(Sprite hub caps had a pressed
"AH" motif), grille with vertical
slats and a central 'MG' badge,
different seat patterns (while MkII
Sprite used MkI seats, MkI Midget
seats had a horizontal bar across
the top of the squab and front of
the cushion and the piping was in a
contrasting colour). Hardtop cars
and those fitted with the optional
sidescreens had a sliding rear as
well as front section to the
'Windshields' sidescreens.

**October 1962. A-H Sprite
'MkII½'. Chassis numbers H-AN7
24732 to H-AN7 38828.
October 1962 M.G.Midget
'MkI½'. Chassis numbers G-AN2
16184 to G-AN2 25767.**
A larger engine of 1098cc capacity
fitted giving 56bhp at 5500rpm.
Crank journal diameters were the
same as those of the 948cc engine
although their length was
increased. Compression ratio was
marginally lower at 8.9:1 and
similar carburettors were fitted with
appropriately different jets.
Improved type gearbox fitted with
much stronger baulk ring
synchromesh replacing earlier cone

type (externally identifiable by
ribbed alloy casing).

Disc brakes were fitted with a
wire wheel option, the stub axle
and bottom kingpin bush being
modified to suit.

Morris Minor type rear wheel
cylinders incorporating handbrake
mechanism abandoned for units
with separate handbrake operation.
Brake shoes adjusted by MGB/Mini
type of backplate adjuster and
consequently brake drums no
longer fitted with adjustment hole.
Disc wheels no longer with
ventilation holes.

Front suspension wishbones
now reinforced with strengthening
gusset.

Sealed beam headlamps
fitted.

External bodywork
modifications: none

Number of trim modifications
carried out involving: revised seats
and dashboard, padded crash rail at
top and bottom of dash, door
casings padded and door tops
padded to match dash crash rail,
carpets fitted instead of mats,
leathercloth inside doors to match
door casings instead of rubber trim,
simulated onyx steering wheel and
grab handle no longer fitted. Smiths
instruments used in place of Jaeger
and a badge fitted to the middle of
the boot (trunk) lid similar to that of
the MGB.

Similar M.G. Midget changes
were made concurrently with those
to the Sprite.

**March 1964. A-H Sprite MkIII.
Chassis numbers H-AN8 38829
to H-AN8 64755**
New 1098cc engine, very similar to
previous unit but substantially
redesigned. Now with 2" main
bearing engine to alleviate 'crank
whip' problem suffered by its
predecessor. Mechanical fuel pump
replaced by SU electric type
situated beneath driver's side (in
UK) rear wheelarch. Mechanical
fuel pump 'mounting' now a solid
casting and the camshaft, with
wider lobes, no longer with fuel
pump cam. Improved inlet manifold

and larger bore exhaust fitted. Gearbox essentially unchanged but subtle changes took place to the internal specifications of the 'ribbed-casing' gearbox throughout its production life (1961-74).

Rear suspension extensively redesigned. Now with half-elliptic rear springing. Different type of rear spring hangers fitted at the front end of the springs while at the rear of the springs, new spring hangers pick up at existing chassis rails with no extra reinforcement necessary. Rear axle essentially unchanged but with different spring attachment points. Rear dampers fitted with larger chambers.

Doors substantially altered. Wind-up windows instead of side screens mean that door pocket space and some elbow room is lost. External door handles and door locks now fitted and opening quarter-lights incorporated. Door shapes slightly altered around the A-post area to accommodate a modified bulkhead top panel which in turn was altered to suit a new wrap-around windscreen which replaced the previous almost flat screen. Hood attached to screen by MGB-type toggle fasteners and the hood shape and hood sticks were modified. Hood tension supplied by the fold-open action of the hood sticks rather than the spring loading found on earlier hoods.

New dashboard with completely revised layout but with same switch and dial functions except key start instead of pull starter switch. Indicator switch now steering column mounted instead of left-right toggle switch mounted on dash. Steering wheel now similar to MGB-style but with only two spokes. Horn push mounted in steering wheel centre embellished with 'Austin' crest instead of the earlier Sprite flash logo.

Trim unchanged from the "MkII½" except that trim colours include blue and red as well as black while red hoods were fitted to red cars. (NB: These were the only Sprites not to be fitted with black hoods as standard.)

March 1964. M.G. Midget MkII. Chassis numbers G-AN3 25788 to 52411.
Identical to contemporary Sprite except price which was £20.00 more in the UK and 170 dollars more in the USA. "M.G." badge mounted in centre of vertically slatted grille. Centre chrome bonnet strips and chrome waist line strips fitted; plain hub caps; "M.G." octagon and the word "Midget" on the boot lid; horn push has "M.G." logo in the centre. Winged "M.G." logo mounted in middle of dash.

October 1966 to late 1969 A-H Sprite Mk IV. Chassis numbers H-AN6 64756 to 79236.
Completely redesigned engine (still A-series) of 1275cc with 'pocketed' block (ie: tappet covers no longer fitted). Timing chain now has double link with two rows of teeth on the sprockets, there is a damper on the front of the crankshaft nose to reduce vibration, the cylinder head is longer and is fitted with larger valves and the radiator and heater outlets are at different angles. From engines 12CD/Da/H1745 (US-market) and 12 CE/Da/H874 (UK-market) the water pump impellers and inlet pipe are enlarged and of greater capacity. Ignition types changed several times during the engine's production run and export cars were often modified to suit local regulations, particularly in the case of US cars. All 1275cc engines have a larger bore but a shorter stroke than their predecessors and

have a higher rev limit of 6300rpm compared with 6000 of the 1098cc engine. Both the car's gearbox and rear axle were unchanged although the rear springs were uprated.

Bodywork changes were based on the rear cockpit area which was enlarged at the expense of the rear bulkhead top panel which became narrower. Small alterations were made to the rear wing tops to accommodate this change. The hood was restyled and fixed to the rear deck and gained an integral folding mechanism replacing the previously fitted fold-up and pack-away type.

Trim was basically unchanged and all cars were fitted with black trim, except for the first few cars which had optional red trim.

Early 1968: Reversing lights fitted as standard. Remote control gearbox turret included reversing light switch. Electrics converted to negative earth but still dynamo generated.

Black plastic 'corporate' B.L. window winder handles fitted and winder mechanism spindle altered to suit. Internal door lock lever broadened and quarter-light catch changed from curved type to flatter, chubbier style. Internal door handle now black plastic.

Eared wheel spinners discontinued on wire wheeled cars and US-style hexagonal spinners fitted.

Late 1968: Revised door casing with different type of material used. Seat upholstery modified; white edge piping replaced by black and seats upholstered with a significantly coarser grained material. Petrol sender unit no longer aluminium top with 6-screw fastening. Now plastic float, pressed steel top flush with top of tank. 3.9:1 differential replaced 4.2:1 unit together with changed speedometer gearing. Oil pressure/water temperature gauge changed from externally illuminated/°F to internally illuminated/°C. Fuel gauge also internally illuminated and with

altered graphics. Crossflow radiator fitted with expansion bottle and different hoses and thermostat housing. This led to relocation of the washer bottle.

October 1966 to late 1969 M.G. Midget MkIII. Chassis numbers G-AN4 52412 to 67637.
As for contemporary Sprite MkIV, except Midget loses central bonnet trim.

October 1969 to late 1970. A.H. Sprite MkIV continues. Chassis numbers H-AN10 85287 to 86766.
October 1969 to late 1971 M.G. Midget MkIII continues. Chassis numbers G-AN5 74886 to 105500.
Rostyle (mag-style) wheels replace plainer disc wheels. Revised recessed black grille. Black sills with chrome strips. Black anodised windscreen surrounds (deleted again after only a couple of months). Slimmer bumpers fitted front and rear with new over-riders. Rear bumper split with number plate situated between bumper halves, number plate lights situated in bumper. Front side lamps lowered to equalise the gap between headlamps and new thinner bumpers. Round plastic boot badge in place of chrome. Front badge now in grille. Winged badge on bonnet deleted. Revised rear lights, 1 piece, squarer pattern, commonised with MGB.

Quieter twin silencer exhaust system with rear box mounted visibly in line with and beneath rear bumper.

Redesigned seats now recliners as standard, not as option. Headrest facility incorporated. Covers of welded vinyl (instead of stitched as previously) with embossed pattern. Revised trim, especially door casings which now have embossed panels. Tan trim with certain body colours. New 3-spoke steering wheels with round holes in spokes. Sprite steering wheels with blank centre, Midget with "M.G." badge. Oil pressure/Water temperature gauge no longer in degrees but marked "Cold-Normal-Hot". Metal gearlever turret with grommet deleted. Replaced by rubber turret completely covered by leathercloth gaiter. Indicator switch incorporating dip switch and horn push. Header rail toggle clips now painted grey instead of chrome and dipping interior mirror windscreen bracket modified for safety reasons.

Early 1970: Courtesy light switches on inner door pillars with light under dashboard. Boot courtesy light fitted. Bonnet and boot fitted with telescopic stays. Uprated heater and integral heater box: heater, motor and blower all in one casing.

January 1971. Austin Sprite MkIV continues. Chassis numbers A-AN10 86802 to 87824.
"Healey" name deleted from Sprite. Front and rear badges modified accordingly. Revised steering wheel with horn push back in centre instead of on stalk. Column locking/ignition key instead of dash mounted. (First modified cars fitted with chrome blanking plug in dash where ignition key was situated. Later dashes modified.)

Sprite discontinued in June 1971.

January 1972 to 1974 M.G. Midget MkIII continues. Chassis numbers G-AN5 105501 to G-AN5 153920.
Rear wheel arches modified to rounded shape, similar to original Sprite. "MkII" Rostyle wheels fitted.

Tumble switches on dash replaced by rocker switches.

Yellow ochre interior trim fitted to certain specific body colours. Better quality carpets fitted. Interior door pull handles now corporate – BL MGB/Marina non-swivelling type. BL gear knob fitted. Steering wheel now with long slots pressed through in place of round holes.

Deeper petrol tank now of 7 gallon (Imp.) capacity. Sender unit now located by internal circlip bayonet ring. Trim of steering rack fitted (of Vitesse/Herald/Spitfire type) with appropriately altered track-rod ends and longer steering arms giving lower geared steering.

1275cc model discontinued in September 1974.

October 1974 to November 1979 M.G. Midget 1500. Chassis numbers G-AN6 154101 to G-AN6 229526.
October 1974: Triumph 1500 engine (specially tuned) and Marina-type all-synchromesh gearbox fitted. Black energy-absorbing bumpers fitted with a return to squarer style of rear wheel arch. Hazard warning lights, door mirrors, anti-roll bar, tonneau cover and rail now standard.

January 1977: Headrests supplied as standard.

April 1977: Inertia reel seat belts fitted as standard.

April 1978: Radio console speaker/radio aerial fitted. 2-speed wipers, cigar lighter and handbrake failure warning light added.

September 1977: Door mirror fitted to drivers' side. Rear axle ratio raised from 3.9:1 to 3.72:1. New facia panel with "M.G." badge deleted. New instruments – commonised with Spitfire. Steering wheel motif now silver on black. New washer jets fitted.

October 1978: Dual line braking system fitted.

November 1979: Last M.G. Midget built.

SPECIFICATION

Please note that the specifications in this section relate to the M.G. Midget MKI and Austin-Healey Sprite MkII on introduction. For production specification changes see 'Evolution'.

Type designation	M.G. Midget MkI and Austin-Healey Sprite MkII.
Built	Abingdon, England, 1961-71 (Sprite), 1961-79 (Midget).
Engine	Cast iron block and head, pressed steel sump, 4-cylinders in-line, overhead valve, camshaft in block. Capacity: 948cc Bore & Stroke: 62.94mm x 76.2mm Maximum power: 46bhp (net) at 5500rpm with 9:1 CR. Maximum torque: 52.8lb.ft. at 3000rpm 2 SU HS2 $1\frac{1}{4}$ inch carburettors
Transmission	Rear wheel drive from front mounting engine. Four speed gearbox with synchromesh on top three ratios, bolted to rear engine plate. Ratios: 3.2:1, 1.916:1, 1.357:1, 1.0:1, reverse 4.114:1, final drive ratio 4.22:1
Body	2-door, 2-seater convertible of unitary construction. Loadings fed into floorpan structure constructed of pressed steel components at John Thompson Motor Pressings, Wolverhampton. Dimensions: Overall height 4ft $1\frac{3}{4}$ inches, length 11ft $5\frac{7}{8}$ inches, wheelbase 6ft 8 inches, ground clearance 5 inches, width 4ft 5 inches, front track 3ft $9\frac{3}{4}$ inches, rear track 3ft $8\frac{3}{4}$ inches, fuel capacity 6 imperial gallons.
Suspension	Front: independent, coil springs. Rear: quarter-elliptic springs.
Steering	Morris Minor rack and pinion, $2\frac{1}{4}$ turns lock-to-lock.
Brakes	7 inch Lockheed drums front and rear, hydraulically operated.
Wheels & tyres	13 inch ventilated pressed steel disc wheels, 5.20x13 tubeless tyres.
Electrical system	12 volt, 43 amp hour battery. Positive earth Lucas dynamo with

tachometer drive to rear. Lucas voltage regulator, coil ignition and wiring harness made up to standard Lucas colour coding scheme.

Performance

Maximum speed, 87mph.
Speed in gears: 3rd gear 68mph, 2nd gear 46mph, 1st gear 28mph.
Acceleration (0-60): 19.6 seconds.
Standing $\frac{1}{4}$ mile: 21.8 seconds.
Acceleration in gears: Top: 20-40mph, 14.4 sec; 50-70, 19.4 sec; Third: 20-40mph, 8.8 sec.; 40-60, 11.3 sec..
Fuel consumption: 32-38mpg.

THE NEW 🅜🅖 MIDGET

THE CAR THAT *Starts ahead*

SPORTING TRADITION

B. M. C. RESOURCES

ABINGDON CRAFTSMANSHIP

New and exciting, the Midget starts ahead of all rivals — with a great and wonderful *tradition* behind it. It "starts ahead" with a superlative brisk performance through the gears that spells safety every time you overtake; it HUGS the road; it corners FIRMLY; it brakes POSITIVELY in the famous M.G. "Safety Fast" tradition. The M.G. Midget of old swept all before it. The new M.G. Midget starts a winner! *Safety Fast!*

WITH A SPORTING APPEAL FROM A SPORTING ANCESTRY

M.G. MIDGET Price £472 plus £197.15.10 P.T. *12 Months' Warranty and backed by B.M.C. Service—the most comprehensive in Europe.*

THE M.G. CAR COMPANY LIMITED, SALES DIVISION, COWLEY, OXFORD
London Showrooms: Stratton House, 80 Piccadilly, London, W.1. *Overseas Business:* Nuffield Exports Limited, Cowley, Oxford and 41 Piccadilly, London, W.1.

ROAD TESTS

MIDGET MILESTONES

M   1929-32   J2   1932-34   PB   1

1961 CARS

MIDGET
returns to
M.G. range

The First Under-1,000 c.c.
M.G. Since 1936

M.G. enthusiasts the world over will welcome the news that, for the first time since mid-1936—when the PB-type Midget went out of production—an under-1,000 c.c. model once again figures in the M.G. range.

The rationalization policy of the British Motor Corporation has been applied to its production and the new Midget is, in fact, one of a pair of basically similar models, the other being the recently introduced Mark II version of the Austin-Healey Sprite. In all their essentials the two cars are identical, but the Midget has a distinctive front, different trim and various de luxe items of finish and equipment not supplied on the standard version of the Mk. II Sprite.

Naturally it costs a little more, the basic price being £472 which, with British purchase tax of £197 15s. 10d., gives a home market total of £669 15s. 10d. This compares with the basic price of £445 (£631 10s. 10d. complete) asked for the Austin-Healey Sprite.

* * *

Power is supplied by a modified 2-carburetter version of the B.M.C. A-type engine, which has now been pro-

duced to the tune of some 1,500,000 units. With a 9/1 compression ratio, it needs 100 octane fuel. The close-ratio four-speed synchromesh gearbox has a central remote-control lever.

Although a conventional rigid axle casing is used, the rear suspension is unusual in employing quarter-elliptic springs in conjunction with parallel, super-imposed radius arms—a system which has the advantages of low unsprung weight and of concentrating the main suspension loading on the centre portion of the unitary-construction shell, the tail playing no part in supporting the weight of the car. The sole functions of the latter are to carry the six-gallon rear tank and provide a useful luggage boot in which the spare wheel is housed horizontally on the floor.

At the front, conventional independent coil-and-wishbone suspension is used, embodying pressed-steel lower wishbones and single forged upper links that also

serve as the arms of the lever-type Armstrong hydraulic dampers. The steering gear is of the rack-and-pinion type.

The Midget has Lockheed hydraulic drum brakes with two leading shoes at the front; the handbrake is on the passenger's side of the propeller-shaft tunnel and has a normal (not "fly-off") ratchet button.

The new Midget is, of course, intended primarily as a two-seater, but there is a considerable space behind the two bucket seats; if required, a cushion can be supplied as an extra to enable this space to be used for carrying a youngster. Otherwise, it can be used for stowing coats, shopping and so on, and it will, in fact, take a good-sized suitcase.

The boot has a lockable lid and straps are provided on the bulkhead to secure the detachable hood material in an envelope clear of the floor. The separate hood sticks (which are of the two-piece type with a joint in the centre for easy stowage)

The hood up, but on the ri which c o

The spare wheel is stowed on the boot floor, but there is quite a fair amount of luggage space by sports-car standards.

Both bucket seats have sliding adjustment and the carpeted well behind them can take extra luggage. Flecked rubber matting covers the front floor. A large rev counter is standard; clutch and brake pedals are of pendant type, the throttle has an organ pedal.

935-36   TA/TB/TC 1936-49   TD 1950-53   TF 1953-55

also have their own envelope and fit round the spare wheel, still leaving a fair amount of room for luggage. With the additional space behind the seats in the passenger compartment, the Midget is very well provided with baggage space by sports car standards.

Unlike so many completely detachable hoods of the past, the new Midget design is neither difficult to erect nor deficient in vision—the latter thanks to a large rear window and sensibly-sized quarter lights, all in transparent plastic of the type which does not suffer from careless stowage. In addition, rigid-framed, sliding-panel side-screens can be fitted to the doors by quick-acting screws which can be operated with a coin. Both the forward and rear Perspex panels are arranged to slide.

The facia board is leathercloth covered, with a padded roll for the scuttle; a revolution counter is standard and both this and the speedometer (with total and trip mileage recorders) have a detailed scale. Other instruments comprise a fuel gauge, a water thermometer and an oil-pressure gauge. Toggle switches are used for the wipers and sealed-beam lights. Other accessories included as standard are a

windscreen washer, anchorage points for safety belts and flasher-type direction indicators.

Among a long list of optional extras available from the factory are a radio set, a tonneau cover which can be arranged to cover the entire cockpit, to protect all but the driver's seat, or to cover the interior luggage space only, a heater and demister, and whitewall or heavy duty tyres; dealer-fitted accessories include a locking petrol cap, a cigar lighter, wing mirrors, twin horns, Ace Mercury wheel discs and a luggage carrier.

Externally, the new model is undeniably a good looker. Points special to the Midget include a very attractive front grille with vertical slats and the traditional M.G. trade mark incorporated in the central vertical bar, and embellishments in the form of a bright metal beading down the centre of the rear-hinged bonnet-top and a full-length flash on the body side; extending from the headlamps to the rear-light clusters, these flashes emphasize the low build. A total of five exterior colours, three types of interior trim and three hood colours are available in combinations which give a total of seven variants.

d provides quite good headroom, and is easy to put the car naturally looks at its sleekest when open, as ght. The picture below shows the special wheel trims n be bought as an extra, carrying the M.G. ctagon, give the car a real *de luxe* appearance.

M.G. MIDGET SPECIFICATION

ENGINE
Cylinders ... 4 in line with 3-bearing crankshaft.
Bore and stroke 62.9 mm. × 76.2 mm. (2.478 in. × 3.0 in.).
Cubic capacity ... 948 c.c. (57.87 cu. in.).
Piston area ... 19.29 sq. in.
Compression ratio 9/1.
Valvegear ... In line o.h.v. operated by push rods and rockers.
Carburation ... Two semi-downdraught S.U. type HS2 carburetters, fed by AC mechanical pump, from 6-gallon tank.
Ignition ... 12-volt coil, centrifugal and vacuum timing control, 14 mm. Champion N5 sparking plugs.
Lubrication ... Tecalemit or Purolator external full-flow filter. Oil capacity 7 pints (incl. filter).
Cooling ... Water cooling with pump, fan and thermostat; 10-pint water capacity (plus ½ pint for heater if fitted).
Electrical system 12-volt, 43 amp. hr. battery charged by 19-amp. generator.
Maximum power 46.5 b.h.p. net (50 b.h.p. gross) at 5,500 r.p.m., equivalent to 2,750 ft./min. piston speed and 2.4 b.h.p. per sq. in. of piston area.
Maximum torque 52.5 lb. ft. at 2,750 r.p.m., equivalent to 138 lb./sq. in. b.m.e.p. at 1,375 ft./min. piston speed.

TRANSMISSION
Clutch ... Borg and Beck 6¼-in. single dry plate.
Gearbox ... Four speeds with direct drive in top; synchromesh on three upper ratios.
Overall ratios ... 4.22, 5.726, 8.975 and 13.504; rev. 17.361.
Propeller shaft ... Hardy Spicer, open.
Final drive ... Hypoid bevel, three-quarter floating axle.

CHASSIS
Brakes ... Lockheed hydraulic, drum type all round.
Brake dimensions Front and rear drums 7 in. dia. × 1¼ in. wide.
Brake areas ... 67.5 sq. in. of lining (33.75 sq. in. front and rear) working on 110 sq. in. rubbed area of drums.
Front suspension Independent by coil springs and wishbones with Armstrong lever-arm dampers.
Rear suspension... Quarter-elliptic leaf springs with parallel radius arms and Armstrong lever-type dampers.
Wheels and tyres Ventilated disc wheels with 4-stud fixing and 5.20-13 tubeless tyres.
Steering ... Rack and pinion.
DIMENSIONS
Length ... Overall 11 ft. 5⅜ in.; wheelbase 6 ft. 8 in.
Width ... Overall 4 ft. 5 in.; track 3 ft. 9¾ in. at front and 3 ft. 8¾ in. at rear.
Height ... 4 ft. 1¾ in.; ground clearance 5 in.
Turning circle ... 32 ft.
Kerb weight ... 14 cwt. (without fuel but with oil, water, tools, spare wheel, etc.).
EFFECTIVE GEARING
Top gear ratio ... 15.4 m.p.h. at 1,000 r.p.m. and 30.6 m.p.h. at 1,000 r.p.m. piston speed.
Maximum torque 2,750 r.p.m. corresponds to approx. 42.2 m.p.h. in top gear.
Maximum power 5,500 r.p.m. corresponds to approx. 84.0 m.p.h. in top gear.
Probable top gear 190 lb./ton approx. (computed by The
pulling power... Motor from manufacturers' figures for torque, gear ratio and kerb weight, with allowances for 3¼ cwt. load, 10% losses and 60 lb./ton drag).

MAKE: Austin-Healey *TYPE: Sprite 1100*

MAKERS: Austin Motor Co. Ltd., Longbridge Works, Birmingham.

THE Motor

ROAD TEST ● No. 47/62

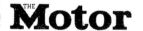

TEST DATA:

CONDITIONS: *Weather: Cool, dry with 10-15 m.p.h. wind. (Temperature 40°-44° F., Barometer 29.6 in. Hg.) Surface: Dry tarmacadam. Fuel: Premium grade pump petrol (98 Octane Rating by Research Method).*

INSTRUMENTS

Speedometer at 30 m.p.h.	9% fast
Speedometer at 60 m.p.h.	6% fast
Speedometer at 90 m.p.h.	4% fast
Distance Recorder	1% fast

WEIGHT

Kerb weight (unladen, but with oil, coolant and fuel for approximately 50 miles)	13½ cwt
Front/rear distribution of kerb weight	54/46
Weight laden as tested	17¼ cwt

MAXIMUM SPEEDS

Mean lap speed around banked circuit	87.8 m.p.h.
Best one-way ¼-mile time equals	92.8 m.p.h.

"Maximile" Speed (Timed quarter mile after one mile accelerating from rest.)

Mean of opposite runs	86.0 m.p.h.
Best one-way time equals	89.2 m.p.h.

Speed in gears (at 6,000 r.p.m.)

Max. speed in 3rd gear	68 m.p.h.
Max. speed in 2nd gear	48 m.p.h.
Max. speed in 1st gear	29 m.p.h.

FUEL CONSUMPTION

54½ m.p.g.	at constant 30 m.p.h. on level
51 m.p.g.	at constant 40 m.p.h. on level
44 m.p.g.	at constant 50 m.p.h. on level
38½ m.p.g.	at constant 60 m.p.h. on level
35½ m.p.g.	at constant 70 m.p.h. on level
28 m.p.g.	at constant 80 m.p.h. on level
21 m.p.g.	at maximum speed of 88 m.p.h.

Overall Fuel Consumption for 1,422 miles, 45.7 gallons, equals 30.8 m.p.g. (9.17 litres/100 km.)

Touring Fuel Consumption (m.p.g. at steady speed midway between 30 m.p.h. and maximum, less 5% allowance for acceleration) 37.2 m.p.g.

Fuel tank capacity (maker's figure) 6 gallons

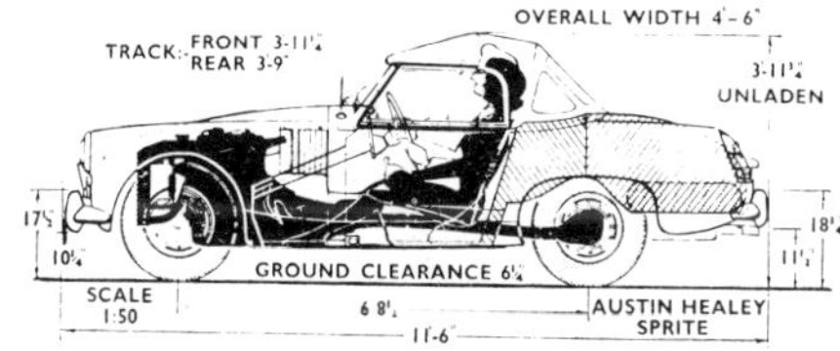
OVERALL WIDTH 4'-6"
TRACK:- FRONT 3-11¼ REAR 3-9"
3-11¾ UNLADEN
17½
10¼
18¼
11½
GROUND CLEARANCE 6¼
SCALE 1:50
6'8¼
AUSTIN HEALEY SPRITE
11'-6"

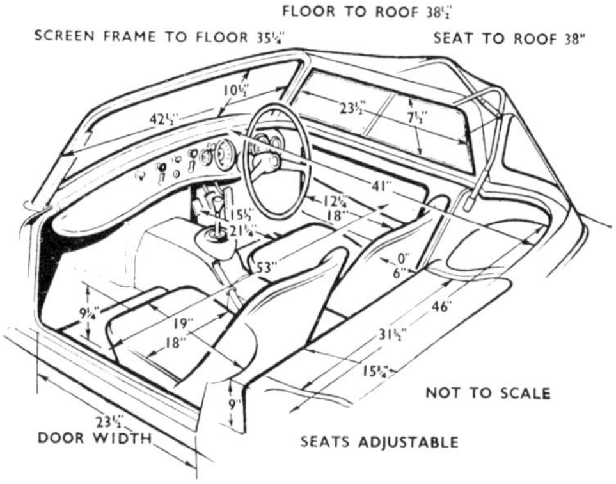
FLOOR TO ROOF 38½"
SCREEN FRAME TO FLOOR 35¼"
SEAT TO ROOF 38"
10½"
42½"
23½"
7½"
41"
12¼
18"
15½"
21¼"
53"
0"
6"
46"
9¼"
19"
18"
31½"
15¾"
NOT TO SCALE
9"
23½"
DOOR WIDTH
SEATS ADJUSTABLE

BRAKES from 30 m.p.h.

1.0 g retardation (equivalent to 30 ft. stopping distance) with 95 lb. pedal pressure
0.80 g retardation (equivalent to 37 ft. stopping distance) with 75 lb. pedal pressure
0.56 g retardation (equivalent to 54 ft. stopping distance) with 50 lb. pedal pressure
0.32 g retardation (equivalent to 94 ft. stopping distance) with 25 lb. pedal pressure

HILL CLIMBING at sustained steady speeds

Max. gradient on top gear	1 in 10.4 (Tapley 215 lb./ton)
Max. gradient on 3rd gear	1 in 6.8 (Tapley 325 lb./ton)
Max. gradient on 2nd gear	1 in 4.8 (Tapley 460 lb./ton)

ACCELERATION TIMES from standstill

0-30 m.p.h.	4.4 sec.
0-40 m.p.h.	7.5 sec.
0-50 m.p.h.	11.1 sec.
0-60 m.p.h.	16.6 sec.
0-70 m.p.h.	25.4 sec.
0-80 m.p.h.	38.3 sec.
Standing quarter mile	20.9 sec.

ACCELERATION TIMES on upper ratios

	Top gear	3rd gear
10-30 m.p.h.	11.4 sec.	7.3 sec.
20-40 m.p.h.	10.8 sec.	7.0 sec.
30-50 m.p.h.	10.5 sec.	7.3 sec.
40-60 m.p.h.	13.0 sec.	8.6 sec.
50-70 m.p.h.	16.3 sec.	11.9 sec.
60-80 m.p.h.	21.9 sec.	— sec.

STEERING

Turning circle between kerbs:

Left	30 ft.
Right	29¾ ft.
Turns of steering wheel from lock to lock	2

B12

Specification

Engine

Cylinders	4
Bore	64.58 mm.
Stroke	83.72 mm.
Cubic capacity	1,098 c.c.
Piston area	20.3 sq. in.
Valves	overhead (pushrods)
Compression ratio	8.9/1
Carburetters	Twin S.U. HS 2
Fuel pump	AC mechanical
Ignition timing control	Centrifugal and vacuum
Oil filter	Purolator or Tecalemit full-flow
Maximum power (net)	55 b.h.p.
at	5,500 r.p.m.
Piston speed at maximum b.h.p.	3,020 ft./min.

Transmission

Clutch	Borg and Beck 7¼ in. s.d.p.
Top gear (s/m)	4.22
3rd gear (s/m)	5.73
2nd gear (s/m)	8.08
1st gear	13.50
Reverse	17.36
Propeller shaft	Hardy Spicer open
Final drive	Hypoid bevel
Top gear m.p.h. at 1,000 r.p.m.	15.3
Top gear m.p.h. at 1,000 ft./min. piston speed	27.9

Chassis

Brakes	Lockheed hydraulic, disc front and drum rear
Brake dimensions	8¼ in. discs 7 in. × 1¼ in. drums
Friction areas	46.7 sq. in. of lining area (13.2 front and 33.5 rear) operating on 190 sq. in. rubbed area of discs and drums
Suspension:	
Front	Independent by transverse wishbones and coil springs
Rear	Live axle and quarter elliptic leaf springs
Shock absorbers:	
Front and rear	Armstrong hydraulic lever type
Steering gear	Rack and pinion
Tyres	5.20-13 Dunlop tubeless

THE MOTOR December 5 1962

719

Austin-Healey Sprite 1100

A more comfortable, livelier version of a popular sports car

CHANGES that were made to the Austin-Healey Sprite on the eve of the recent Motor Show received comparatively little publicity at a time when there was heavy pressure of motoring news. Briefly it may be recalled that an increase in engine size from 948 to 1,098 c.c. raised the maximum power from 46.5 to 55 b.h.p. at the same r.p.m. (5,500), that the clutch was enlarged in diameter by one inch, the gearbox acquired the latest baulk ring synchromesh and disc brakes were fitted to the front wheels. These alterations alone have endowed the Sprite with a much better all-round balance of mechanical virtues but in fact development has not stopped here; the latest model is quieter, smoother, better trimmed and equipped, has more comfortable seats and yet it still remains the lowest priced production sports car on the British market.

Latest Developments

ENGINE enlargement has been effected partly by a small increase in bore and partly by a new longer stroke crankshaft very similar to that used in the ADO 16 models. Indeed, the upper part of the engine is virtually identical with that of the M.G. 1100 saloon and except for a narrow range vibration period

Above: Externally there is nothing to distinguish the new 1,100 c.c. Sprite from its predecessor. *Below:* When not in use the hood and its separate folding frame can be removed altogether and stowed in the boot.

at about 4,800 r.p.m. which causes some gearbox chatter, a stiffer crankshaft makes it very smooth all the way up to maximum r.p.m. An orange sector on the rev. counter extends from 5,500 to 6,000 r.p.m. and a red sector from 6,000 to 7,000; in performance testing we treated 6,000 r.p.m. as the limit except for a small excursion into the red to record a 50-70 m.p.h. time in third gear.

This engine has a very long range of handy torque; it pulls strongly from under 20 m.p.h. in top gear and covered the useful 30-50 m.p.h. range in only 10.5 sec. against 13.6 sec. for the previous model. It starts extremely easily and warms up fairly quickly although low-speed pick-up remains very sluggish until a proper running temperature is approached. The heater becomes effective with remarkable rapidity even in very cold weather, delivering large quantities of hot air long before the thermometer needle has moved off its stop. A simple push-pull control regulates the temperature and a quiet fan can be used to boost the air flow at low speeds. However, if this is used in heavy traffic, a fresh air intake mounted low down in the nose very soon fills the cockpit with fumes from the exhaust pipes of vehicles in front.

From outside, the Sprite still has a healthy bark from the exhaust but from inside both exhaust and mechanical noises are more subdued and it seems appreciably quieter and less fussy than previous models. At high speed, however, a dominating wind noise makes conversation very trying at speeds above 60-70 m.p.h. and restricts enjoyment of the radio mainly to town and suburban motoring. Noise apart, however, there is little

In Brief

Price (as tested) £485 plus purchase tax £101 12s. equals £586 12s.

Capacity	..	..	..	..	1,098 c.c.
Unladen kerb weight		..	..	..	13½ cwt.
Acceleration:					
20-40 m.p.h. in top gear ..			..	..	10.8 sec.
0-50 m.p.h. through gears		..	..	..	11.1 sec.
Maximum top gear gradient		..	..	..	1 in 10.4
Maximum speed		..	..	..	87.8 m.p.h.
"Maximile" speed	..	..	..	..	86.0 m.p.h.
Touring fuel consumption		..	..	..	37.2 m.p.g.
Gearing: 15.3 m.p.h. in top gear at 1,000 r.p.m.					

sense of mechanical strain when cruising in the 70-80 m.p.h. region.

A mean maximum speed of 88 m.p.h. was recorded in conditions which were not very favourable with a one-way speed approaching 93 m.p.h. on the downward leg of the circuit. The larger engine has improved the maximile speed much more than the maximum, suggesting that it is now perhaps a little under-geared and that, at 5,700 r.p.m. in top, power has started to fall away. Using the gears acceleration is remarkably good for a 1,100 c.c. car, 50 m.p.h. being reached from rest in 11.1 sec. and the standing start quarter mile completed in 20.9 sec. A clutch which gives a firm positive take-up but which is smooth enough to discourage wheelspin when dropped in at high r.p.m. was a help in recording these excellent figures.

Nearly 30 m.p.h. can be reached in the high bottom gear; a re-start on a 1 in 4 gradient was accomplished easily but a marginal success was recorded on 1 in 3 only by slipping the clutch at high r.p.m. for a considerable distance—an abuse which the previous smaller clutch would not have accepted. The hand-brake held the car on these gradients but many drivers will regret that it is not a fly-off type; in the off position it disappears between the seats. The new gearbox has the close well-chosen ratios which first appeared on the 948 c.c. Mk. 2 model and the same smooth, light, positive change but the baulk ring synchromesh is no longer beaten by extremely rapid shifts. First gear is not synchronized and there is some transmission roughness at certain speeds on the overrun. Reverse gear is particularly easy to engage rapidly by a natural movement backwards and towards the driver against a spring gate loading which is quite light—an ideal arrangement for driving tests.

Light, sensitive handling

THE rack and pinion steering is outstanding for quick manoeuvring. With a 30 ft. turning circle, 2¼ turns of the wheel take it from one lock to the other and it is so light that this manoeuvre can be accomplished easily with one hand. There is a certain amount of initial roll on entering a corner which appears to be accompanied by side float of the car on its quarter-elliptic rear springing. This results in a tendency to lurch rather eagerly into a swerve in a manner suggesting strong roll oversteer; in fact, however, once set up for a corner the Sprite stabilizes and sits down very firmly until ultimately the rear wheels begin to break away gently and progressively. A little more air in the back tyres postpones the final breakaway to even higher speeds.

With these characteristics the car can be flicked through a series of fast bends with little more than a few movements of the wrists by a natural and experienced Sprite driver who will probably regard most other cars as sluggish and unresponsive. Heavy-handedness is not compatible with the handling characteristics and a clumsier driver with slower reactions may well regard the steering as over-sensitive.

For a sports car the ride is certainly not harsh or heavily damped and on main roads it is comfortable but the rear suspension has a limited travel so that bad roads soon bring the limiting stops into operation. Sometimes, especially with a light load, a succession of bumps will induce back axle hop and the car will deviate momentarily from its straight course but on corners, when the springs are laterally loaded, this effect is largely suppressed and the rear wheels hold the road very well. The pressed steel chassis structure feels stiff and sturdy and there are very few rattles.

The Sprite has always been notable for a very good driving position and this has now been further improved by seats with much thicker and softer upholstery which still give adequate support against cornering forces and which, although perhaps a little upright, remain comfortable on really long runs. These remarks must be qualified, however, in the case of tall drivers; most people 5 ft. 10 in. tall or more will have the driving seat as far back as it will go and very tall people or those who have particularly long legs may find the steering wheel jammed against their thighs and the pedals difficult to operate. Clutch and brake are well separated but the latter is so close to the side of the body that even a size 8 shoe may be caught between the two. Heel and toe operation of brake and organ type accelerator is easy and straight-forward.

Austin-Healey Sprite 1100

Above: There is little change in the appearance of the enlarged engine and its accessories. Except for the distributor and fuel pump most of the parts are easy to get at. *Above right:* The wide, meshed radiator grille contrasts with the clean, simple lines. *Right:* The boot is the only part of the Sprite that can be kept under lock and key. Although the hinges intrude on the useful vertical height there is room for a large suitcase on top of the spare wheel.

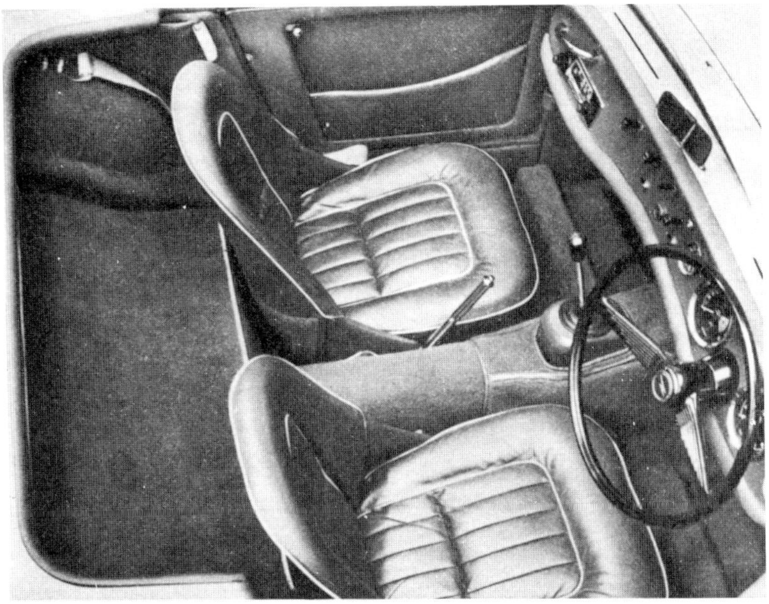

THE MOTOR 721
December 5 1962

A padded roll along the bottom edge of the dashboard improves the appearance considerably although some drivers thought it made the interior look smaller. Very tall drivers found their left leg in contact with the loudspeaker housing, just out of sight under the facia. The photograph also shows the excellent seats, the handbrake which lies rather inaccessibly in the horizontal "off" position and the carpeted space behind the seats which comfortably houses a carry cot.

The 7 in. drum brakes fitted to previous models had little margin for abnormally fast driving; 8¼ in. discs are now used at the front and these are lighter to use and inspire considerable confidence when stopping really hard from speeds near the maximum.

Improved trim

At one time the interior of the Sprite was trimmed in somewhat spartan fashion by comparison with its close relative the M.G. Midget but now it is very well padded and fully carpeted. Luggage space in the small but useful lockable boot is supplemented by the space behind the front seats; with these seats moved forward a notch or two it proved possible to carry one extremely uncomfortable adult passenger in this position even with the hood up.

There are no locks on the doors and no exterior handles; in damp frosty weather the sliding plastic side screens froze in their guides and it was then necessary to unbutton part of the hood to reach the inside door catches. At speed these screens tend to pull outwards under wind forces and there are noticeable draughts particularly round the driver's right hand. From the point of view of wind noise and weather proofing they are not to be compared with winding glass windows but they do allow the use of hollowed-out doors which give a great deal of elbow room and have large and extremely useful rigid pockets. There is no facia cubby hole or ash tray.

Visibility is good, a large wrap-round flexible rear window preventing any feeling of being cramped or shut in. A low sloping bonnet gives an excellent close-range view of the road ahead that should be particularly valuable in fog but the mirror tends to cut off the driver's view of the near side wing without giving particularly good rear vision. A larger shallow mirror would give adequate spread in elevation and make better use of the width of the rear window. With the hood down, of course, the all-round view is superb but a back-draught in the open cockpit discouraged much open motoring in the very cold weather which persisted for most of our test. The hood is easy to raise or lower single handed and it is sufficiently well tensioned to prevent much flapping at speed.

It seems a pity that non-cancelling indicators are still fitted although the warning light is a prominent one. A more serious criticism, perhaps, is the small range given by a 6-gallon tank and a fuel consumption in the region of 30 m.p.g. The steady speed m.p.g. figures show that the Sprite is not inherently an extravagant car and it could be driven very economically indeed by anyone who was so minded, but our test staff were more inclined to enjoy its sporting qualities to the full and to drive it as fast as it would go with continual use of the delightful gearbox. Unlike the previous model, the test car did not need 100 octane fuel, there being no trace of pinking on premium grade.

Fundamentally, the Sprite design has changed little since its introduction and not surprisingly it now has rivals which can outshine it in some directions, notably perhaps in rough road performance, but at £586 it now offers even more remarkable value for money than before. Above all it still remains great fun to drive.

Coachwork and Equipment

Starting handle	No
Battery mounting	On the scuttle under the bonnet
Jack	Bipod screw type with ratchet handle
Jacking points	Below centre of body on either side
Standard tool kit: Wheel brace, hub cap remover, plug spanner and tommy bar.	
Exterior lights: 2 headlamps, 2 sidelamps, 2 stop/tail lamps, number plate lamp.	
Number of electrical fuses	2
Direction indicators	Non-cancelling flashers
Windscreen wipers	Twin blade electric
Windscreen washers	Manual pump type
Sun visors	None
Instruments: Speedometer (with total and decimal trip mileage recorders), rev. counter, fuel gauge and combined oil pressure/water temperature gauge	
Warning lights	Generator, main beam, direction indicators
Locks:	
With ignition key	Ignition only
With other keys	Boot
Glove lockers	None
Map pockets	One in each door
Parcel shelves	None
Ashtrays	None
Cigar lighters	Optional extra
Interior lights	None
Interior heater	Optional extra fresh air heater and demister
Car radio	Optional extra
Extras available: Radio, heater, tonneau cover, laminated screen, hard top, cigar lighter, heavy duty tyres, twin horns, luggage carrier, etc.	
Upholstery material	PVC
Floor covering	Carpet
Exterior colours standardized	6
Alternative body styles	None

Maintenance

Sump	6½ pints, S.A.E. 30 (summer) or 20 (winter)
Gearbox	2¼ pints, S.A.E. 30
Rear axle	1½ pints, S.A.E. 90 hypoid
Steering gear lubricant	S.A.E. 90
Cooling system capacity	10 pints (2 drain taps)
Chassis lubrication: By grease gun every 3,000 miles to 12 points.	
Ignition timing	5° b.t.d.c.
Contact breaker gap	0.014-0.016 in.
Sparking plug type	Champion N5
Sparking plug gap	0.024-0.026 in.
Valve timing: Inlet opens 5° before t.d.c. and closes 45° a.b.d.c.; exhaust opens 51° before b.d.c. and closes 21° a.t.d.c.	
Tappet clearances (hot): Inlet 0.012 in.; exhaust 0.012 in.	
Front wheel toe-in	0-⅛ in.
Camber angle	1°
Castor angle	3°
Steering swivel pin inclination	6½°
Tyre pressures:	
Front	18 lb.
Rear	20 lb.
Brake fluid	Lockheed (S.A.E. 70 R 3)
Battery type and capacity	12-volt 43 amp. hr.

MG Midget 1500

1,493 c.c.

Smallest British Leyland sports car given much more punch by bigger engine. Quick, accurate steering but handling throttle-sensitive and inclined to oversteer. Harsh ride, excessive wind noise with hood up. Undergeared. Limited range

The Midget rolls considerably when cornered hard and the outside front wheel becomes heavily loaded as seen here. If at this point the steering wheel is held steady the car increasingly oversteers as the corner continues; lifting off the accelerator causes the tail to twitch sharply outwards

THERE was an outburst of lamentation from MG enthusiasts when the Midget 1500 was announced, apparently because the A-series engine had been replaced by a Triumph-designed unit. From an engineering point of view the change was almost inevitable. The Midget needed a bigger engine to counteract the effect of safety and antipollution equipment in America, where it sells in its greatest numbers; and at 1,275 c.c., the A-series unit was at the end of its "stretch potential". The answer was to instal the Triumph engine which, while of similar design and vintage, had long ago been given a longer stroke to bring its capacity to 1,493 c.c., its first application being the now-defunct front-drive Triumph 1500.

The purists may decry the move, but Triumph is a name long respected in the sports car business and there is no reason to suppose the Spitfire engine should be unsuitable for the Midget. It might be more in order to complain that a considerable increase in swept volume has resulted in a negligible increase in quoted power, from 64 bhp (net) to 66 bhp (DIN). On the other hand torque, a more important part of a sports car's character than most people realize, is increased by a greater margin. Against all this has to be balanced the greater weight of the new car, with a kerb weight (our measurement) of 15·3cwt compared with the 13·8cwt of the last 1,275 c.c. Midget we tested.

Performance and economy

The proof of the Midget 1500 is in the stopwatch, and there is no doubt it is substantially quicker than the late-series 1,275 c.c. car. Comparisons are valid because the final drive ratio remains unchanged at 3·9 to 1; the adoption of the single-rail "corporate" gearbox has meant some change in internal ratios, which are wider than before. Tyre size likewise remains the same.

The Midget 1500 is a genuine 100 mph car, and this represents a great advance on the 1275 which managed only 94 mph mean when tested in 1971. Unfortunately maximum speed takes the car over the red line on its rev counter, which over-reads by a modest 100 rpm at maximum speed; clearly, therefore the Midget is substantially undergeared to make best use of its peak power, which falls at 5,500 rpm. Higher gearing would not only improve economy, but also permit higher speeds in the intermediate gears.

Although we ran the Midget beyond the 6,000 rpm red line to attain its ultimate maximum speed, we stuck to the limit in the lower gears with the result that first gear would not quite take the car to 30 mph, and third stopped just short of 70 mph. Our figures point up the considerable gap between second (47 mph maximum) and third, which is felt on the road to some extent but is disguised by the spread of useful torque.

Open sports cars always suffer in performance at the top end when they are run with the hood down, and the Midget was no exception. Lowering the hood took the maximum speed down to 94 mph – apart from making life very uncomfortable at that speed. We took no acceleration figures with the hood down, but there is no doubt they would be inferior to those obtained with the hood in place.

MG Midget 1500

All the Midget 1500 acceleration figures are far superior to those of the 1275, whether from a standing start or in any particular gear. Standing starts are best accomplished without a surfeit of revs and sudden engagement of the clutch, which tends to produce strong and uncomfortable axle tramp. A more gentle procedure, feeding in the clutch fairly fast from a 2,000 rpm starting point, trims half a second off the 1275 time to 30 mph, giving a respectable 3·7sec to this speed. The 1500 proceeds to 60 mph in 12·3sec (a 1·8sec improvement), and to 90 mph in 35·3sec, a better time by no less than 16sec. In like fashion, the standing quarter-mile now takes 18·5sec compared with 19·6 before.

In the gears, every single feature claimed by the 1275 is bettered by a substantial margin. Not only is the torque curve flatter; the 1500 does not run out of breath so quickly at the top end, while flexibility is improved to the extent of being able to pull away from 10 mph in top, which the 1275 would not tolerate.

Comparisons

Performance

ACCELERATION SECONDS

True speed mph	Time in Secs	Car Speedo mph
30	3·7	30
40	5·8	40
50	8·5	50
60	12·3	61
70	17·0	71
80	24·0	82
90	35·3	92
100	—	102

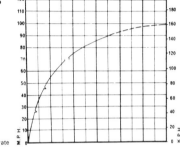

Standing ¼-mile
18·5sec 72 mph

Standing kilometre
34·9sec 90 mph

Mileage recorder: accurate

GEAR RATIOS AND TIME IN SEC

mph	Top (3·90)	3rd (5·58)	2nd (8·23)
10–30	9·8	6·2	3·9
20–40	9·2	5·8	4·0
30–50	8·7	5·8	—
40–60	9·6	6·7	—
50–70	10·2	7·9	—
60–80	12·5	—	—
70–90	19·3	—	—

GEARING
(with 145–13in. tyres)
Top ....16·44 mph per 1,000 rpm
3rd...........11·50 mph per 1,000 rpm
2nd .... 7·79 mph per 1,000 rpm
1st........... 4·82 mph per 1,000 rpm

MAXIMUM SPEEDS

Gear	mph	khp	rpm
Top (mean)	101	163	6,140*
(best)	102	164	6,200*
3rd	69	111	6,000
2nd	47	76	6,000
1st	29	47	6,000

*See text

BRAKES
FADE (from 70 mph in neutral)
Pedal load for 0·5g stops in lb

1	35	6	45–65
2	40–45	7	50–65
3	40–60	8	50–65
4	45–65	9	50–65
5	45–55	10	50–60

RESPONSE (from 30 mph in neutral)

Load	g	Distance
20lb	0·22	137ft
40lb	0·46	65ft
60lb	0·70	43ft
80lb	0·96	31ft
Handbrake	0·33	91ft
Max Gradient	1 in 3	

CLUTCH
Pedal 42lb and 4¾in.

Consumption

FUEL
(At constant speed – mpg)

30 mph	48·8
40 mph	44·5
50 mph	39·2
60 mph	34·2
70 mph	29·8
80 mph	26·2
90 mph	22·1
100 mph	17·6

Typical mpg 30 (9·4 litres/100km)
Calculated (DIN) mpg 32·5
          (8·7 litres/100km)
Overall mpg 27·9 (10·1 litres/100km)
Grade of fuel: Premium, 4-star (min 97RM)

OIL
Consumption (SAE 20W/50) 1,000 mpp

TEST CONDITIONS:
Weather: Fine
Wind: 0·3 mph
Temperature: 15deg C (58deg F)
Barometer: 29·95in. Hg
Humidity: 65 per cent
Surface: Dry concrete and asphalt
Test distance 883 miles

Figures taken by our own staff at the Motor Industry Research Association proving ground at Nuneaton.

Dimensions

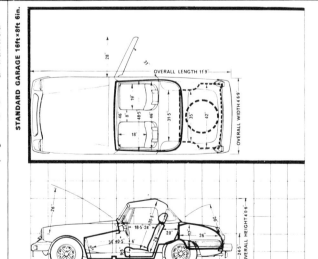

STANDARD GARAGE 16ft x 8ft 6in.

OVERALL LENGTH 11'9"
OVERALL WIDTH 4'6"
OVERALL HEIGHT 4'0·5"

GROUND CLEARANCE 5"
WHEELBASE 6'8"
FRONT TRACK 3'10·3"
REAR TRACK 3'8·75"

TURNING CIRCLES:
Between kerbs
L, 30ft 10in.; R, 31ft 11in.
Between walls
L, 32ft 2in.; R, 33ft 3in.
Steering wheel turns, lock to lock 2¾

WEIGHT:
Kerb Weight 15·4cwt (1,720lb–780kg)
(with oil, water and half full fuel tank)
Distribution, per cent
F, 53·7; R, 46·3
Laden as tested:
18·0cwt (2,020lb–917kg)

Super Profile

Where economy is concerned, one might expect the 1500 to be less economical because of its larger engine. On the other hand its fuel economy should at least be comparable, because the car remains the same size and there is no reason why any more power should be needed to push it along. Two factors upset this tidy calculation. One is that the Midget in its new form is a good deal heavier; the other is its extra performance, which is used some if not all of the time. As a result, our overall fuel consumption emerged as 27·9 mpg compared with 29·6 mpg for the smaller-engined car. This is not a particularly good figure – worse than the Spitfire 1500 for instance, but then the Spitfire has higher gearing and, for our test, overdrive as well. It was noticeable, though, that the Midget's consumption stayed almost constant whoever the driver and whatever the journey, and at no time did it record a brim-to-brim figure of better than 30 mpg.

This is not to say that 30 mpg is unattainable. Our steady-speed figures show that cruising at a constant 60 mph (with the hood up!) enables the driver to better that figure with ease. If this limit were observed and fierce acceleration avoided, the Midget would prove quite economical; but it is not inherently so, still less the way it is likely to be driven.

Handling and brakes

The Midget sticks to its simple suspension arrangement with double wishbones at the front

Specification   MG Midget 1500

FRONT ENGINE, REAR-WHEEL DRIVE

ENGINE
Cylinders	4, in line
Main bearings	3
Cooling system	Water; pump, fan and thermostat
Bore	73·7mm (2·90in.)
Stroke	87·5mm (3·44in.)
Displacement	1,493 c.c. (91·1 cu. in.)
Valve gear	Overhead: pushrods and rockers
Compression ratio	9·0 to 1. Min octane rating: 97RM
Carburettors	2 SU HS4
Fuel pump	SU mechanical
Oil filter	Full-flow, replaceable cartridge
Max power	66 bhp (DIN) at 5,500 rpm
Max torque	77 lb. ft. (DIN) at 3,000 rpm

TRANSMISSION
Clutch	Diaphragm-spring, 7·25in. diameter
Gearbox	4-speed, all-synchromesh
Gear ratios	Top 1·0
	Third 1·43
	Second 2·11
	First 3·41
	Reverse 3·75

Final drive	Hypoid bevel, ratio 3·90 to 1
Mph at 1,000 rpm in top gear	16·44

CHASSIS AND BODY
Construction	Integral, with steel body

SUSPENSION
Front	Independent: double wishbones, lever arm dampers, anti-roll bar
Rear	Live axle, semi-elliptic leaf springs, lever-arm dampers

STEERING
Type	Rack and pinion
Wheel dia	15½in.

BRAKES
Type	Disc front, drum rear
Dimensions	F 8·25in. dia R, 7·0in. dia, 1·25in. wide shoes
Swept area	F, 135 sq. in., R, 55 sq. in. Total 190 sq. in. (211 sq. in./ton laden)

WHEELS
Type	Pressed steel Rostyle, 4-stud fixing, 4in. wide rim
Tyres – make	Pirelli Cinturato (on test car)
– type	Radial ply tubeless
– size	145–13in.

EQUIPMENT
Battery	12 volt 40 Ah.
Alternator	28 amp a.c.
Headlamps	Sealed beam, 120/90 watt (total)
Reversing lamp	Standard

Electric fuses	4
Screen wipers	Single-speed
Screen washer	Standard, manual plunger
Interior heater	Standard, water valve type
Heated backlight	Not available
Safety belts	Static type
Interior trim	Pvc seats
Floor covering	Carpet
Jack	Screw pillar type
Jacking points	One each side
Windscreen	Toughened
Underbody protection	Phosphate treatment under paint

MAINTENANCE
Fuel tank	7 Imp gallons (32 litres)
Cooling system	7½ pints (inc heater)
Engine sump	8 pints (4·5 litres) SAE 20W–50. Change oil every 6,000 miles. Change filter every 6,000 miles
Gearbox	1·5 pints. SAE 90EP. Check every 6,000 miles
Final drive	1·75 pints. SAE 90EP. Check every 6,000 miles.
Grease	8 points every 6,000 miles
Valve clearance	Inlet 0·010in. (cold) Exhaust 0·010in. (cold)
Contact breaker	0·015in. gap.
Ignition timing	10deg BTDC (stroboscopic at 650 rpm)
Spark plug	Type: Champion N9Y. Gap 0·025in.
Tyre pressures	F 22; R 24 psi (normal driving) F 26; R 28 psi (high speed) F 22; R 26 psi (full load)
Max payload	420lb (190kg)

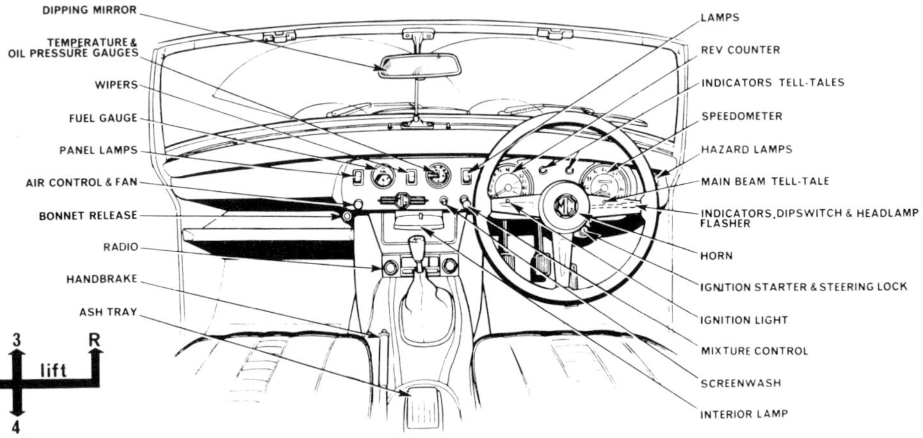

Dashboard and controls diagram with labels:

DIPPING MIRROR, TEMPERATURE & OIL PRESSURE GAUGES, WIPERS, FUEL GAUGE, PANEL LAMPS, AIR CONTROL & FAN, BONNET RELEASE, RADIO, HANDBRAKE, ASH TRAY, LAMPS, REV COUNTER, INDICATORS TELL-TALES, SPEEDOMETER, HAZARD LAMPS, MAIN BEAM TELL-TALE, INDICATORS, DIPSWITCH & HEADLAMP FLASHER, HORN, IGNITION STARTER & STEERING LOCK, IGNITION LIGHT, MIXTURE CONTROL, SCREENWASH, INTERIOR LAMP

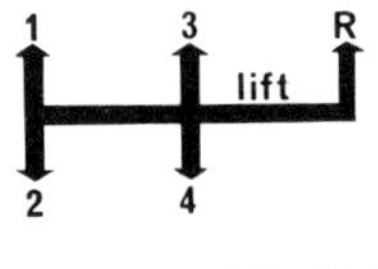

Gear shift diagram: 1 3 R / lift / 2 4

Servicing

6,000 miles

Time Allowed (hours)	3·5
Cost at £4.30 per hour	£15.05
Engine oil	£2.50
Oil Filter	£2.15
Air Filter	£1.08
Contact Breaker Points	£0.52
Sparking Plugs*	£1.48
Total Cost:	**£22.78**

*when required

Routine Replacements:	Time hours	Labour	Spares	TOTAL
Brake Pads – Front (2 wheels)	1·00	£4.30	£3.80	£8.10
Brake Shoes – Rear (2 wheels)	1·35	£5.80	£3.80	£9.60
Exhaust System	0·85	£3.65	£19.50	£23.15
Clutch (centre+driven plate)	8·00	£34.40	£12.83	£47.23
Dampers – Front (pair)	1·55	£6.65	£28.88	£35.53
Dampers – Rear (pair)	1·00	£4.30	£25.52	£29.82
Replace Half Shaft	0·55	£2.35	£13.80	£16.15
Replace Alternator	0·70	£3.00	£27.00	£30.00
Replace Starter	1·60	£6.90	£15.86	£22.76

42

AUTO | MG Midget 1500

and a live rear axle located by semi-elliptic leaf springs with no other form of assistance. It worked well enough in the past, given the Midget's very limited wheel travel, but there are signs that the latest car needs something more sophisticated to cope with its greater torque and performance.

Part of the trouble lies in the fact that the Midget, like the MGB, has been given increased ride height at the back to compensate for the greater weight of its "5 mph" bumpers and associated structure. As a result, roll stiffness at the back end has been reduced and there is much more tendency to oversteer. This is despite the heavier tiny but constant corrections he engine which means the front wheels bear a greater part of the total weight.

The best feature of the Midget, as always, is its very quick and accurate steering. With less than three turns of the wheel between extremes of an average 32ft turning circle, the driver never has to tie his arms in knots to turn a corner or rescue a situation. Inevitably, there is some kick-back on rough surfaces, but this is by no means the most tiring feature of the car.

Straight-line stability is no better than average, except on ultra-smooth surfaces. Normally, the Midget feels willing enough to keep to a straight course but if the wheel is released for a moment it soon reveals its willingness to wander off-line. The feeling of stability is actually due to the driver

Massive front bumper makes the whole car look bigger than before; inset lights are well protected by lipped extensions. Door mirrors are part of standard equipment. Headlamps are sealed-beam units, not halogen

Standard number plate is mounted beneath the new "5 mph" bumper, rather than below the boot lid as in previous Midgets. Reversing lights are standard and boot lid can be left unlocked if the driver wishes

being barely conscious of the tiny but constant corrections he is applying.

The handling, as we have already said, holds the promise of oversteer. It is not evident at first, for in gentle driving the Midget stays very close to neutral. When driven harder into a corner, if the driver holds the wheel and accelerator steady, the tail will come out steadily until some of the lock has to be paid off before the car gets too sideways. In itself this is no bad thing, for it enables the Midget to be driven in distinctly sporting fashion by someone who knows what he is doing. At the same time it holds the seeds of danger for anyone less clever.

The real snag to the Midget's handling in 1500 form lies in its sensitivity to the throttle. Given the previous situation where the car has been wound hard into a long, tight bend, any sudden release of the accelerator will bring the tail out very smartly, calling for opposite lock to pin it down. Again, this is a situation beloved of some drivers but it means the Midget is much less predictable, and certainly calls for more skill, than many small saloons of equal performance *and* cornering ability. The drawback is compounded by limited roadholding, which can leave the car well-balanced fore and aft, but skittering sideways onto a wider line than desired. Despite the increased weight and torque, the tyre section remains the same at 145–13in., and it is difficult to avoid the conclusion that the 1500 is somewhat under-tyred.

In the wet, the roadholding is considerably reduced and the Midget tends to skate around on smooth-surfaced corners. In this case, however, it is much more forgiving and the quick

steering really comes into its own.

The brakes need moderate effort and generally work well, giving a well-controlled ultimate stop of 0·95g for a pedal effort of 80lb – well within reasonable limits. The brakes have good "feel", with no sign of sponginess, and no tendency to snatch when cold. Their fade performance is less reassuring with a near-doubling of effort for a 0·5g stop during our ten-stop test, and some smell of linings towards the end; but even then there is no increase in pedal travel.

The handbrake works well, our test car recording a 0·33g stop when the handbrake was used alone on the level. It also held the car well facing either way on the 1-in-3 test hill, on which a restart was easily achieved thanks to the low first gear – but not without a smell of clutch lining.

Comfort and convenience

The Midget could hardly be described as anything but cramped, with difficult entry and exit. It has always been so, and buyers have accepted it. But the statistics tell us that Britons are getting bigger – not to say Americans – and we are surely approaching the point where it may be too small for its own good. In fact our largest staff members (the largest of all scaling 16½ stone and 6ft 2in.) found the interior space just sufficient with the driver's seat moved to its back stop, but complained of their inability to shift position to relieve numb spots. More serious were the contortions involved in getting in and out, even with the hood down.

The seats do not look especially inviting, reminding one of the shapeless BMC equipment of a few years ago. This is doing them less than justice. Together with the generally tight confines of the interior they locate driver and passenger well, and they do their best to damp out the effects of the generally mediocre ride. The ride itself will not disappoint Midget enthusiasts and could only be described, euphemistically, as "good for the liver". The limited wheel travel and high spring rates give the Midget no chance of offering a comfortable ride and the result is misery when the car is driven quickly on any uneven surface, let alone a really rough one. On the credit side it is very rare for the suspension actually to bottom, and the 1500 is notably free of the crashes and bangs which afflicted some earlier Midgets, especially when their dampers were past the first flush of youth. Nor is the handling very much affected by suspension movement, so a driver fit enough to withstand the battering can make rapid progress along almost any British road.

Bigger Triumph 1500TC engine does not look unduly large under Midget bonnet, with plenty of length to spare and room for the massive heater trunking. Access to some items is good, but others (such as battery behind heater blower unit) are difficult to reach

Above: Black crackle-finished facia panel gives slightly vintage air to the interior. Rev counter and speedometer are widely separated but can still be seen inside rim of large steering wheel. Minor dials are less easily read

Left: Midget seats look rather stylized but not very well shaped; in fact they are quite comfortable, damping out the worst effects of the ride, while the small size of the interior ensures good location. Note the awkwardly-placed door handle by the occupant's shoulder

Boot lid is supported by a single self-locking strut. Capacity is strictly limited and there is a low sill over which luggage must be lifted. Spare wheel and fuel tank lie flat on the boot floor and beneath it respectively

The controls are not well laid out, but at least they are easy to understand and are clearly labelled. There are signs of penny-pinching in the single (too slow) speed wipers, the manual-plunger washer, the primitive heater control. Of the major controls, the steering wheel is larger than one might expect and close to the chest by modern standards; the pedals are understandably close together in their narrow tunnel. Clutch effort is high but pedal movement limited, though the clutch takes up sweetly enough. In the test car, however, the accelerator linkage was rather "sudden" and no help to gentle driving. The gearchange is precise but not as quick as some of its rivals.

A major drawback of the Midget is its high interior noise level. For the most part it is made up of wind noise, which drowns the other components to the extent where one is unsure how much contribution the engine is making until one switches off and coasts at high speed. The wind noise itself comes from the hood, and while this may seem inevitable there are other soft-top cars which do not suffer in the same way (or at least, not to the same extent). In the Midget's case it is noticeable that the car is much quieter with the hood down, and the radio easier to hear, at speeds as high as 70 mph. Indeed, with the hood up the radio is almost inaudible above this speed. The engine actually makes a lot of noise at higher speeds – it simply can't compete with the wind roar. Induction and exhaust noise is high when the car is accelerating hard, at anything over 5,000 rpm; but when the car is driven more gently the 1500 unit is quiet and refined. Noisy or not, it is very smooth right up to the red line and beyond, in a way that may surprise MG diehards.

Even with the hood up, visibility is not bad. At first sight the windscreen is shallow but it seems to provide sufficient view for short and tall drivers; the hinged quarter-lights obstruct the front-quarter view a little, but the "over-the-shoulder" blind spot is cleared by two extra windows let into the hood. Two door mirrors are standard, but on the test car they continually flopped down to a useless position. The wipers clear only a small area of screen and are too slow to cope with heavy rain. Sealed-beam headlights give good illumination at night but the driver's low eyeline prevents him making the most of it. Reversing lights are standard.

The heater is a primitive affair with a single push-pull control for temperature, and a single-speed fan which can only be switched on when full heat is selected. There is no means of selecting airflow to screen or floor, the output being shared arbitrarily. However, the fan is quiet and the heater clears the screen quickly even in humid conditions. There is no direct-flow ventilation other than via the quarter-lights.

Living with the Midget 1500

By comparison with Midget hoods of a few years ago that of the 1500 is easy to contend with. It is not yet a simple one-handed operation either to stow or erect it, though, and in particular it is much easier to fit its leading edge to the windscreen rail if four hands are available. With the hood down one does not get too battered by the airflow, even at high speed, but one driver found that when driving open in light rain the inside of the windscreen soon became covered in droplets and the occupants of the car dampened.

A basic appeal of the Midget is its simplicity, and this is still so with the 1500 which is no more difficult to work on than its predecessors. The most awkward servicing point is the need to reach the battery at the very rear of the engine compartment under the hinge line of the bonnet; the dipstick is not easy to find, especially in the dark. A link with tradition is the need to attend to eight grease points during the 6,000-mile service – but there are no intermediate service intervals, so an average car requires only twice-a-year attention.

A main drawback of the car is its small (7-gallon) tank, which gives a safe range of less than 200 miles. It is filled via a simple cap in the rear panel, and unlike many modern tanks can be filled quickly to the brim with no danger of blow-back.

There are few accessories to be added to the Midget from the MG option list. A hardtop is expensive but might prove an investment in terms of reduced wind noise and long-journey comfort, wire wheels are available for those who can face the chore of cleaning them; and head restraints may be specified. There is no overdrive option, far less an automatic. Static seat belts are standard – apparently there is no room for inertia-reel units.

In conclusion

There is no doubt that the performance of the Midget has been greatly improved by its change of engine, and there is now a spread of torque which allows the car to be driven sportingly or to be lugged along all the way in top gear by a lazy or tired driver. At the same time the handling has suffered in some respects and the car is no longer as predictable or forgiving as it was.

People are bound to differ on how badly cramped they find the interior (though few will argue with the infuriating difficulty of reaching the interior door handles, but few would quarrel with the conclusion that the ride is harsh and the noise level over-high.

Now that the Midget and the Spitfire share the same engine, the question of their joint survival must arise. For our money – and there is scant price difference between the two – the Spitfire is much more practical and civilized. There will always be those who will scorn it for precisely those reasons, but if further rationalization comes to pass it will be difficult to make out a case for the Midget *vis-à-vis* its stablemate. □

MANUFACTURER:
British Leyland UK Ltd., Austin-Morris Division, Longbridge, Birmingham

PRICES			
Basic	£1,333.00	Insurance	Group 5
Special Car Tax	£111.08		
VAT	£115.53	**EXTRAS (inc VAT)**	
Total (in GB)	**£1,559.61**	Wire wheels	£56.12
Seat Belts, static type	(standard)	Hard top	£112.09
Licence	£40.00	Head restraints*	£18.27
Delivery charge (London)	£15.00	*Fitted to test car	
Number plates	£6.60		
Total on the Road (exc insurance)	**£1,621.21**	**TOTAL AS TESTED ON THE ROAD**	**£1,639.48**

OWNER'S VIEW

Lindsay R. Porter interviews James Thacker. James is an M.G. Car Club member and is well known in Club circles for his highly competitive racing Midgets.

L.R.P: Why are you so interested in Spridgets?

J.T: I bought my first in 1968; a 1963 MkII with a 1098 engine. In those days there was nothing to compare with them. Second-hand, they cost about the same as a Mini so they were the right price but of course they had the huge advantage that they were open. On top of that you could say that there was nothing that someone with common sense and a workshop manual couldn't do when they went wrong.

L.R.P: But there were other inexpensive sports cars aound at the time …

J.T: There's no competition! The Midget is for someone who likes driving. The Spitfire is for people who like looking. You never see *them* being raced.

L.R.P: What sort of Spridget do you own now and when and why did you buy it.

J.T: My present road car is a 1974 Midget, an 'N' reg; one of the last with the chrome bumpers and a real engine. I bought it in Birmingham, where I live, in April 1980, after an awful lot of searching.

L.R.P: Why was finding the right car such a problem? There are so many about!

J.T: Yes, but there's an awful lot of rubbish about too! I followed up quite a large number of advertisements from the *Evening Mail* but not one of the cars was what it seemed. The most common fault I found was corrosion around the spring hangers at the rear of the floorpan, though there were lots of other faults on display as well, such as more rot around the A-pillars and weak front dampers. The condition of the dampers is really critical to the handling of these cars. They're so easy to control largely because they have soft springs and stiff damper settings which makes handling progressive and very controllable. It also gives the dampers a lot of work to do.

Eventually I heard of 'my' car through the grapevine. My brother-in-law had a solicitor friend who wanted to sell. He heard I was looking – and there we were. I got it at the right price too!

L.R.P. What sort of condition was it in?

J.T: It didn't need any welding; that was critical because I don't have access to welding equipment. It did need some mechanical work but as I've said, that's no problem. The discs were rusty – they're another trouble spot. They're rather thin so they frequently need replacement. They're prone to warping too. The front wheel bearings had gone and the fuel gauge, temperature gauge and horn all needed replacement. I seem to remember that one of the kingpins had had it too. The car certainly wasn't immaculate but then, it didn't need to be; it suited me down to the ground. The rear silencer was holed and I quickly replaced the double silencer system with a single box system of the 1967 era – to make it sound like a Midget again and not like a boring bog-standard Mini!

L.R.P: I know that you are pretty quick on the track. Have you modified your road car at all?

J.T: I can't resist carrying out just a bit of tuning work. Although I've done nothing dramatic to the car I have made it more into the sort of car that suits me personally. The engine on my car was in good condition when I bought it, so I did no more than to fit a Leyland Special Tuning 567 cam which is actually the same cam as that fitted to the old 998cc Mini-Cooper. It gives longer valve opening times – about the same as an MGB – but with no higher lift. That way, you don't lose anything but you do in fact gain more torque. I can't think why they never fitted the cam as standard. Incidentally, I wouldn't ever advise anyone to buy a re-profiled cam; they're never as good. Stick to the real thing! I fitted a Cooper 'S' distributor to go with it, of course.

Other mods rapidly fitted included a rear telescopic damper conversion. Mine was the prototype for the Spridgebits conversion, by the way. I've also fitted a Motalite 13 inch steering wheel, a long centre-branch exhaust manifold and an Aley roll-over bar. The standard driver's seat won't go back far enough nor recline enough to give you a comfortable driving position with the roll-over bar in place so it was necessary to fit a bucket seat just to get a decent driving position.

L.R.P: Have you had many problems with the car?

J.T: Not really. The Midgets and Sprites are really incredibly reliable. Just to give you an idea, my racing car engine only received two rebuilds in ten years of really hard racing, apart from having a new oil pump and bearings fitted every year as a routine measure.

One problem which I did encounter when removing my rear dampers was that you just can't get a spanner of any description on the top damper bolt to stop it turning while you remove the nut. It's such a pig to get off that it's a good enough reason in itself to change to teles!

L.R.P: Do you have any problems in obtaining parts?

J.T: None at all, except that the competition clutches I use on my racing cars are no longer available. When the cars were still being made I used to buy my spares from Patrick Motors, a B.L. dealer in Birmingham. These days I get all of my stuff from Spridgebits partly because they sponsor my track car and so I get everything at a special price but also because they really do carry a fantastic range of parts for Midgets and Sprites.

L.R.P.: What kind of performance and handling does the car have?

J.T: My car has got a bit more responsiveness and a bit more torque that the standard Midget but even so, the standard 1275 engined car is about as good in a straight line as a Midget 1500. The cornering is better than just about anything on the road, though. It's very predictable and you would have to be very silly indeed to spin it. The handling is also quite superb. On the road it's just like driving an extension of yourself.

L.R.P: Have you ever entered any of your Spridgets in a Concours.

J.T: Certainly not! Concours competitions don't appeal to me at all. Midgets and Sprites are for driving, not for looking at.

L.R.P: Perhaps you would like to tell me something about your involvement with motor sport?

J.T: Well, to start at the beginning, I bought a Midget MkIII in 1969 which I raced in Sprints with the M.G. Car Club. I had a lot of axle tramp which caused first gear to strip — and when I say strip, well, the teeth came out of the drain plug! I replaced it with a guaranteed reconditioned unit and immediately did the same again. I took it back to the reconditioners with an innocent look on my face and they said they'd never seen anything like it. I said nothing!

Then, in late 1970, I bought TZA 238 which was a rather special car, ex-Alec Poole. Actually it came to me via Alec's brother Arnie. The car was a somewhat modified Frogeye with an 1150cc short stroke engine — a real screamer — modified along the lines of the 1071 Cooper 'S'. I raced it from 1971 to 1977 but in '77 the car was written off. I lost my brakes and when I tried to put the car sideways to stop it, I rolled and completely wrecked the car. As much as possible was salvaged from the wreck and it was rebuilt as a Midget. This time it has a 1293cc engine and rose-jointed suspension, and ten inch wheels with Formula II slicks. The rear end is detachable and the suspension arrangements in general are somewhat revolutionary!

Overall, I have competed in well over a hundred competitions in Midgets and Sprites — mainly circuit races at Silverstone, Mallory Park, Brands Hatch, Oulton Park, Donington etc. and also at a few Sprints and Hillclimbs. I have managed to win over sixty awards for 1st, 2nd or 3rd places.

L.R.P.: That's an impressive record, how easy is it for a newcomer to break into motor sport?

J.T: The M.G. Car Club have circuit events for tyros which they call high speed trials. Here you are given a target of so many laps in a certain time so that you are not racing against others but only against your own ability. It gives an ideal opportunity to get the feel of racing.

I should say here that there are two distinct types of racing in which Midgets can take part. First there's Production racing in which standard wheels and tyres and relatively few modifications are

made and Modified racing where much wider wheels, fibreglass bodywork and all sorts of extensive modifications are allowed. It goes without saying which is the dearer to start off with.

But back to the beginners, M.G. Car Club members can race in closed-to-club meetings, as I did when I began, which are very small meetings where road cars can be raced. Lots of people race just once a year at these meetings while others go on to more competitive racing.

L.R.P: The M.G. Owners Club now run race meetings too, don't they?

J.T.: Yes but I don't know much about them except that their lap times are much slower. I've never been an Owners Club member.

L.R.P: Do you find it worthwhile to be a Car Club member?

J.T: Yes, because they enable me to go racing! I joined in 1966 when I owned a T.F; in those days they had a very strong T-series section. I don't think they've kept up with the times quite as much as they might which is why the Owners Club is now so much bigger but you get a fair monthly magazine and of course, the Car Club suits me.

L.R.P: What advice would you give to the potential Midget or Sprite owner?

J.T. Well, I run mine mainly because it's a cheap way of running a second road car. But Midgets are also terrific fun to own, so it's important to look for a good one. The engines are pretty archaic but very robust so the main things to look for are the areas that I looked for when I was buying my present road car. As to which model to go for, my advice to potential owners would be to go for the latest 1275cc cars with a good shell. I don't recommend going for an earlier car simply because the bodyshell is less likely to be sound and I don't recommend the later, 1500 cars because the increased ride height means that they don't corner as well and because the engines themselves aren't tuneable; that engine has already been taken as far as it can go.

On top of that, the round-arched cars are prettier to my mind. I was told by someone at B.L. that they only went back to the squarer shape because by the time they had jacked the body up, the round arches looked silly.

L.R.P: In short, how would you sum up the benefits of owning the Midget?

J.T: It's got its disadvantages. It's a bit small, even for someone like me, who is not all that tall. Getting in and out can be a bit uncomfortable, too. On the other hand, it's very manoeuvrable and with good springs and dampers, it still

outcorners everything else on the road. On the track, it's absolutely remarkable. Its *average* speed at Mallory or Thruxton is 95 which gives it the same performance as the purpose built single-seaters of the fifties mainly because of its cornering. The safety limits built into the production cars' hubs were phenomenal — enough to take 10 inch wheels without modifications.

In the end, what it boils down

to on the road is good performance, good handling and predictable cornering. It's got to have the best performance-to-money ratio on the road!

BUYING

Which model?

The Midgets and Sprites sold extremely well in both the UK and the USA and the enthusiast looking for a car should have no difficulty finding them freely available in the local and national press for the foreseeable future. Buying one of the first that becomes available, even if in good condition would not be wise until a decision has been made about which model to go for. The difficulties arise because although there is a strong continuity of character which extends right through the range, hardly any components at all could be transposed directly from a 1961 Midget onto a 1979 car or vice versa without changing the car's correct specification. In fact the car metamorphosed gradually but considerably from a primitive, hard-sprung roller skate to a car that had learned to move up a class; a more sophisticated, slightly less hard-sprung roller skate! It became a kind of Midget Thermidor, the insides removed, mixed with a little smooth cream and poured back into the same shell. But the cream makes a lot of difference!

Fortunately, in all but a very few cases, the manufacturer's chassis numbers and Mark changes reflect the changes actually carried

out to the cars. As a result it is a simple matter to trace the cars' development model by model with comments on the pros and cons of each from the enthusiast's point of view.

The first car or cars covered by this book are the Midget MkI and Sprite MkII. For some enthusiasts, the appeal of the M.G. marque has made it always more desirable than the Sprite but on the one hand all cars (all but a tiny handful of Cowley-built cars) hail from Abingdon, the home of M.G., while on the other hand the *first* Sprite was an Austin-Healey and it could be argued that it is this marque name that is the more 'pure' – "You pays yer money", as they say. And indeed the difference in cost was the greatest difference between the cars when new. The Midget had slightly more padding in the seats and a small number of other trim differences but cost around 5% more than the Sprite. In essence, the MkI Midget/MkII Sprite, is a "Frogeye" with altered bodywork. The effects of the body changes are to make the cars rather more "usable" than their predecessor: it is not so unusual to see a couple with a small child on the rear 'shelf' at a club meeting, the boot stowed full of picnic gear. Everything in the boot is as accessible as with any other orthodox car while the nipper *can* be stowed in the rear of the cockpit – though he or she may complain if it happens too often. It really isn't

at all comfortable, especially since these cars have the Frogeye's quarter-elliptic rear springs which have limited travel and give a hard ride. Spares for these rear suspension systems are not difficult to get hold of, although main dealers no longer stock the parts, of course; it is necessary to go to a specialist who stocks parts specifically for the earlier cars. One of the biggest weaknesses with these cars is the relatively weak crankshaft fitted to early 1098cc cars. Potential problems should have shown themselves by now, but check that an earlier problem has not led to the transplant of a 'wrong' engine. From this point on there are few mechanical problems to be encountered except for front suspension wishbone bushes which can seize and which then often require replacement of the whole wishbone assembly. Otherwise, mechanical longevity is one of the most appealing features of all the cars.

Midgets and Sprites from 1964 to 1974 are fundamentally the same car. For the first two years, a 1098cc engine was still fitted but in terms of smoothness and power, the subsequent 1275cc engine is a much better bet. All the cars were fitted with the sort of refinements that make them much more usable than the pre-1964 cars. They all had half-elliptic springing which gave more comfortable suspension while the road holding did not deteriorate. The addition of wind-down windows lost some elbow room but gained a great deal in convenience and the lockable doors added peace of mind. The hood fitted at the same time as the 1275cc engine, in 1966, is one of the best sports car hoods around being very easy to fold up and down – another point in that car's favour. Other minor trim and body changes took place before 1974 but none were hugely significant. See 'Evolution' for details.

In late 1974, dramatic changes were made which added

greatly to the car's ease of use. A larger Triumph engine was fitted which gave little more in terms of top speed but added a lot more flexibility. The Marina gearbox gave the valuable benefit of synchromesh on first gear and the black bumpers and raised ride height altered the car's looks and handling to a small extent. With their additional trim and longer spring travel, these cars are undoubtedly the most comfortable of all the Sprites and Midgets.

What to check

While Sprites and Midgets are relatively simple to repair, the cost, especially of body repairs, can be quite high in relation to the value of the cars. The first place to look on all models is the rear of the floorpan area. The quarter-elliptic cars are particularly prone to taking a hammering in that area. Slide the seats forwards, lift the mats and give the whole area close scrutiny with the aid of an inquisitive screwdriver. Repeat the performance from beneath the car in the same vicinity.

Another vital structural point is the sill area. Both outer and inner sills are prone to the most dreadful rust attack and outer sills, especially, should be checked with a magnet for the presence of camouflaging filler. With magnet still at the ready, rear wheel arches should be tested for 'botching' and so should the leading edge of the bonnet.

Door pillars are another notorious rot-spot and when corrosion in this area takes a hold the bottom door hinge very embarrassingly breaks away leaving the door flapping like a sail. On cars with wind-up windows, doors themselves are prone to rotting out. First place to look is along their bottom faces with the doors open. Usually this area goes well before the vertical faces are attacked.

The front suspension, as already mentioned, can be mildly expensive to repair but most mechanical parts are so inexpensive and commonplace that they are far less important than the car's structural condition.

Interestingly, a warning from a British motoring organisation, the AA, claims that F, G and H registration Spridgets (in the UK), ie 1967 to 1970 cars, "did not have under-wing or underbody compounds applied during manufacture and consequently show a fair amount of corrosion of underfloor pressings and frame members."

Moreover, they go on to say that, "when the electrocoat-painted body protection started in late 1970 a marked improvement in corrosion resistance was soon accomplished." These pre-1970 cars were found to have a higher than average incidence of corrosion in doors, rear wings, jacking points and floor, all of which were improved on later cars. It's all quite a long time ago now, in motoring terms, but it could be worth bearing in mind if you want a car with the minimum of repair work carried out on it.

Review of value patterns

Even the best success stories often don't start off as such. When the MkI Sprite was first built, comments passed upon its shape were rarely favourable. After a little while, it began to be regarded with amused tolerance while the cars current status as a 'classic' could hardly be imagined without its startlingly distinctive appearance. This point is made to illustrate a fundamental trap for those assessing the appeal and thus the value of cars whose time has not yet arrived. Cars which may seem to have no appeal now can become highly sought after – not because they change, of course, but because the circumstances which surround

them alter. It must always be remembered that the last one hundred E-type Jaguars *did not sell*. What price one of those exotic black beauties nowadays?

In a similar sort of way, the last M.G. Midgets took a long time to sell. They were not specially prepared, like the last E-types or MGBs and so they have no special status now save that of being those with the best chance of being well preserved by virtue of their age. When the "Mark" of car to which they belong was introduced in 1974 with its rubber bumpers, raised ride height and Triumph-derived engine, the beaters of chests and brows were well at it, declaiming the car as having lost the spirit of the true Austin-Healey or M.G. Only those who enjoyed the new cars' extra comforts voted their approval by actually going out and buying one, while those who delude themselves into thinking there is a true faith to keep never will accept it. However, with the passing of the open-topped small car and the substitution of the M.G. Metro, the latest Midget looks as much an acceptable sports car as any of its predecessors. Well served by spares of all types, it can be expected to appreciate within the next few years as the supply of traditional sports cars in general runs out.

The last Sprites and M.G. Midgets, with 1275cc engines, are likely to benefit from an even more prolific supply of engine and gearbox spares as many of their mechanical components were shared with so many other cars. In the foreseeable future, these models are likely to remain one of the cheapest ways of going 'Spridgeting'. They offer a reasonable turn of speed but still lack refinements such as synchromesh on first gear.

The Austin-Healey Sprites MkIII and IV and the M.G. Midgets MkII and III are likely to remain afflicted by the neither fish nor fowl syndrome – except that they are all very pleasant little sports cars in their own right and it could very well be that demand for a sports car with the qualities of character, simplicity (especially compared with the electronic black boxes on wheels yet to come!) and running economy, will cause distinctions between the different marques to merge. To return to the example of E-type Jaguars, the lack of supply of these virility symbols has caused price differentials between ages and types of the cars to become eroded. For different reasons, the same could well happen to these cars with the result that price differences between the "Marks" could become greatly diminished.

Austin-Healey Sprites MkII

and M.G. Midgets MkI have been left until last because it is likely that whatever happens to prices in the rest of the range, the scarcity of these cars and their structure (Frogeyes without the frogeyes but with most of the endearing little crudities) will ensure that they will command the highest prices in the long term. This will be because enthusiasts who know what they are talking about will go for one of these cars as a kind of second-

string Frogeye (whose prices are likely to reach T-series M.G. levels by the way) while those not "in the know" won't know the difference between these and the later cars. It could make for some interesting hunting in years to come ...!

CLUBS, SPECIALISTS & BOOKS

Of course, a good deal of a Sprite's or Midget's attractiveness comes from the pleasure it gives to the person sitting in the driver's seat. But the lone pleasures of owning, maintaining, restoring and driving a 'Spridget' are multiplied several times over when those pleasures and the experiences of them can be shared with others and when a little more can be learned about the car. The best way of meeting like-minded enthusiasts is by joining the appropriate one-make club which provides meetings, competitions and shows for the enthusiast to attend and which is the best source of all for practical, down to earth information on running the car. And not only will there be social and practical benefits from 'joining the club', there will probably be financial ones too, saving the membership fee several times over.

Clubs, services and books are details in the following list with, after each one, a brief résumé of what it has to offer. There are, of course, others, but those shown below are those which are most well known and which, in the author's opinion, have most to offer the Sprite or Midget owner.

Clubs

To join the **Austin-Healey Club**

send an sae to Ms Carol Marks, 171, Coldharbour Rd., Bristol BS6 7SX, England. The Club is also split into various area registers, information on which can be obtained from the above. The British club should also be able to provide information on overseas Austin-Healey clubs.

The **Austin-Healey Club of America** can be contacted at 705 Dimmydale Road, Deerfield, Illinois 60015, USA.

The **M.G. Owners Club,** a lively and enthusiastically run large club with a free monthly magazine also caters for Sprites. It gives special offers on spares and tools, and there are both national and local meetings. Good system of 'Recommended Suppliers' scheme operated and trade discounts for members at every B.L. dealer. Address: M.G. Owners Club, Roche Bentley, 13, Church End, Over, Cambridgeshire, England.

M.G. Car Club: Direct descendant from original, factory-supported club. Excellent for racing connections. Polished monthly magazine with good historical, technical content. Secretaries for areas and also for most models of M.G. Not commercially minded. M.G. Car Club, Assistant Secretary – Sheila Lawrence, 67 Wide Bargate, Boston, Lincolnshire PE21 6LE, England.

In the United States, **The American MGB Association,** surprising though it may seem, also caters for Midgets. Excellent quarterly magazine and technical advice service. Address: AMGBA, P.O. Box 11401, Chicago, Illinois 60611, USA. (UK Chapter: Ken Smith, Broomhill Villa, 185 Broomhill Road, Old Whitington, Chesterfield, England.)

Specialists

University Motors (USA). Prop: John H. Twist. Mail order service, excellent technical know-how, full workshop facilities. University Motors Ltd, 614 Eastern Avenue S.E., Grand Rapids, Michigan, 49503, U.S.A.

Spridgebits Ltd. Props: Grahame Sykes and Jed Watts. 'Spridget' specialists, as their name suggests. Carry a wide range of mechanical and body spares (including repair panels). Full workshop facilities. Nothing too much trouble! Spridgebits Ltd. (Mailing Address), 54 Saint Peters Road, Handsworth, Birmingham B20, England (Telephone 021 554 2033).

Sprite & Midget, B, C, V8 Centre Specialists in 'Spridget' parts with a full range of mechanical and body spares (including repair panels). Full workshop facilities. Friendly and helpful. Sprite & Midget, B, C, V8 Centre, 22-28 Manor Rd, Richmond, Surrey TW9 1YB, England.

Austin-Healey Spares Ltd. Prop: Fred Draper (once Healey Car Co). Storeman. Courteous and friendly. A-H Spares Ltd, Unit 7, Westfield Road, Southam Industrial Estate, Southam, Warwickshire CV33 0JH, England. (Telephone 0926 817181).

The Classic Restoration Centre, the author's own body shop. The

Centre specialises in Midgets, Sprites and MGB and it draws on Lindsay's considerable knowledge of the cars. Full range of body and mechanical parts also available.

Lifesure Ltd. Specialists in providing car insurance for classic cars of all types, especially for Agreed Value policies where the car's value is agreed in advance rather than left to the 'low-book' values that normally prevail. Lifesure Ltd, 34 New Street, St. Neots, Huntingdon, Cambridgeshire PE19 1NQ, England. (Telephone 0480 74604/75148).

Books

"Sprites and Midgets – Guide to Purchase & D.I.Y Restoration" by Lindsay Porter. Gives a clear and thorough guide to every aspect of buying, running and restoration, including all bodywork repairs, of every model of Sprite and Midget. Published by G.T. Foulis/Haynes in 1983.

"More Healeys" by Geoffrey Healey. The genuine inside story of Frogeye development and production. Strong on fact and anecdote and easy to read. Published by Gentry/Haynes.

"The Sprites and Midgets" by Eric Dymock. Concise guide in the "Collector's Guide" series. Usual sense of *déjà vu.* Published by Motor Racing Publications, London.

M.G. Midget & A-H Sprite Owners Workshop Manual. A complete guide to all mechanical repairs to all models. Published by Haynes.

PHOTO GALLERY

1. This Tickford-bodied Healey is typical of the cars which the Warwick-based Healey company was offering shortly after the war. Most Healeys were Riley-powered and offered elegant road versions of cars with a rally and track background.

2

3

2. The Austin and Healey companies learned about collaboration through the "Big" Healey range and went on to produce the nippy, eccentric, fast selling Frogeye Sprite in 1958.

3. After the Frogeye Sprite came the Sprite MkII and the Midget. Abingdon was responsible for the Farina-influenced rear end while Healey sculpted the front. This is an early prototype - front wing lines were lowered before production. (Photo: courtesy B.L. Heritage).

4. This early publicity shot shows clearly that it is impossible to cram very much into a Midget boot. Still, its improved accessibility was one of the main reasons for adapting the Frogeye rear end. (Photo: courtesy B.L. Heritage).

5. An early accessory was this wheel trim set with lots of mock ventilation holes echoing those on the disc wheels beneath.

6. Early original 2-spoke Austin-Healey steering wheels are now quite rare, particularly when complete with the correct badging in the horn push at the wheel centre.

4

5

6

7

8

9

10

11

12

7. Sprites were relatively unadorned when compared with their Midget sisters. The "cheese-grater" grille was chosen as being distinctively different from the early Midget's grille.

8. Somehow the vertical grille bars on the Midget suited the car so much better and the chrome strips on bonnet and body side-panels added an unostentatious touch of brightwork to what was essentially sober bodywork (Photo: courtesy Malcolm Green).

9. Undoubtedly the bonnet line of the new car was "cleaner" than that of the Frogeye but it was also less characterful. Note the winged badge on the bonnet, missing from later cars.

10. At the back, the car was very much like the MGB, which was to follow a year later. Development of the new body's outer panels cost as much as the development of the complete Sprite MkI bodyshell, completed only a few years earlier.

11. The "new" car's hood was redesigned to fit the changed body shape. Tonneau clips are seen to be in plentiful supply!

12. Hood tension was still facilitated by use of spring loaded clips. just as on the earlier Sprite ...

13

14

15

16

13. ... but the one-piece hood stick could no longer be stored in the rear cockpit because of the new body shape, so hood sticks had to become splittable.

14. Later Frogeye-type sidescreens were fitted in conjunction with the same type of windscreen. Fitted to this car is a rare period accessory - an external door opener, which was never fitted as part of the original specification.

15. The earlier type of radiator was continued in use with these cars, the only visible difference being the invisibility of the radiator front, now obscured by steelwork.

16. Rear suspension was by Frogeye-type quarter-elliptics with all that that implies: twitchiness, hardness but, some say, less roll when cornering fast.

17. Electronic tachometers were still not in BMC's hit

parade so the old Smiths-Lucas double act continued to be mounted on the rear of the dynamo giving cable drive to the rev. counter.

18. Apart from the alloy rocker box, this Sprite MkII engine bay is quite original. The heater is the same as in the Frogeye days but note the twin plastic-capped $1\frac{1}{4}$ inch SUs with Coopers element-type air cleaners and also the primitive emission control on the inlet manifold - the shape of things to come!

17

18

19. The original Sprite's rear end had already been strengthened by a box-section which snaked its way across the rear-axle tunnel, close against the wheel arch. This, and its supporting structure, were enough to support rear spring hangers when Sprites and Midgets were converted to half-elliptics. All that was added was a cut-away box-shaped supporting bracket.

20. Inevitably, the transverse engine layout so popular at BMC was the basis for a proposed new sports car. This unlovely prototype - almost a sports car version of the "land-crab" 1800 - thankfully never made any further progress. (Photo: courtesy B.L. Heritage).

21. Anti-roll bars were optional at one point but became standard later. Front suspension remained of the A30 type throughout the car's production life.

22. Some owners hankered after the superb accessibility of the Frogeye and fitted aftermarket one-piece fibreglass bonnets like this dramatically styled example.

23. Lack of power saw the engine increased from 948 to 1098 then 1275cc. This 1968 Midget is remarkably similar in appearance to the MkI but had both torque and 'pep' added to its other superb driving characteristics.

19

20

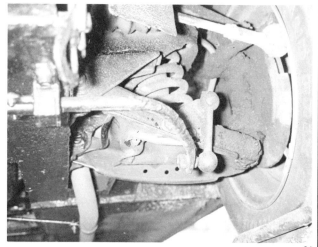

21

22

23

24

25

24. Inside the car, extra comfort could be found to go with the wind-up windows. This paddle operates the seatback reclining mechanism.

25. As on so many Midgets, the original steering wheel has been replaced by an accessory wheel. In 1968 dash layout was still comparable with that of the early Midget.

26. In 1969 came the car's first facelift. This US-market model had side markers and all cars received black

grilles and sills. At first, screen frames were black coated but this quickly peeled and the original finish was restored to production models! (Photo: courtesy B.L. Heritage).

27. The new recessed grille with chrome strip certainly made the car look a little meaner. New, slimmer bumpers meant that sidelamps had to be repositioned downwards to equalise the bumper-sidelamp-headlamp gap. Rubber inserts were added to the over-riders.

28. The black sills with straight chrome strip were meant to make the car look lower and sleeker and to take the emphasis away from the kick-up at the front of the sill, designed originally to fit the Frogeye bonnet. (Photo: courtesy Malcolm Green).

29. At the rear, the MkIII was fitted with split bumpers and squarer rear lamp lenses à la MGB. The rounded wheelarches echoed the lighter style of the original Frogeye rear end.

26

27

28

29

30

31

30. The optional speaker console is fitted to this car, just below the dash. Note the steering wheel with slots in the spokes.

31. Door mounted drivers' mirrors were fitted to these post-facelift cars. Chrome side strips were no longer fitted so many owners have added their own pin stripes like those of this car.

32. The car's new exhaust system was much quieter - less sporty, some thought - and received an extra silencer. There was no room within the existing pipework so it was fitted across the rear of the car.

33. Under the bonnet so much seems familiar although just about everything has altered in some detail. The under bonnet heater tap was a strange anachronism by this time. (Photo: courtesy Malcolm Green).

34. The gearbox tunnel still had an upward extension but it was now hidden under a plastic mock-leather gaiter. An interior light was now fitted.

35. A little later, the steering wheel became of the type shown here and the M.G. badge disappeared from the dash to be replaced by the anonymous interior lamp.

32

33

34

35

36

37

36. Quarterlight handles were now of the more comfortable, and probably safer, flat type, similar to those fitted to the MGB.

37. Although quite characterful, the Midget was still a mass-produced car and some owners still had to go to some lengths to personalise their cars. Otherwise this door trim is quite original.

38. Suedette seat covers were never standard but headrests were an optional extra. Oblong holes were provided in backrest tops to facilitate their simple fitting.

39. To return to the earlier cars for a moment, the correct bonnet pull is round and has a "B" in the centre.

40. Later pulls were mounted in exactly the same place but were fitted with a T-handle. Heater/cold air flaps still directed air into the footwells.

41. The easy folding hood was made to look very neat when folded by clipping the standard cover into place.

38

39

40

41

42

43

42. Inclement British weather makes a tonneau cover essential - this one is fitted with pockets to accommodate headrests. With the heater blower turned on and tonneau cover in place a warm glow can be directed to the nether regions, even in cold weather!

43. On the other hand, the Californian sun can make it too hot to take the top down. Then a zip-out rear screen adds a welcome through draught.

44. The chunky looks of the rear end are really quite attractive although from some angles that exhaust pipe can look rather obtrusive.

45. Some consider the round wheelarch, chrome-bumpered Midget to be the most attractive of all; they certainly stand a good chance of becoming the most collectable in the long run. (Photo: courtesy Malcolm Green).

46. These Frogeye wheels are the same as those fitted to the following Sprite and Midget models–or at least, those without wire wheels ...

47. ...while "MkII" Rostyles like these were fitted to the post-facelift cars.

44

45

46

47

48

49

48. Many proud owners fit these chromed Rostyles which are easier to keep clean than the painted variety and do not become scruffy so easily.

49. Midget racing within the M.G. Car Club and also the M.G. Owners' Club is very popular. Here James Thacker circulates in a ProdSports GRP-bonneted Midget he once co-owned.

50. James has moved up in the M.G. Car Club racing world as he explains in the 'Owner's View' section of this book. He is fortunate in having his garage/workshop at home.

51. James' 1293cc Midget is a ModSports car - in other words a Midget that has been developed about as far as it can go while retaining a few of the car's basic characteristics and components.

52. James' Midget is seen here with front spoilers and rear aerofoil which, he says, make a great difference to aerodynamics. Following James around Silverstone's Woodcote Corner is a 3.5-litre MGB V8 – it isn't catching up!

53. The engine, although based upon a standard block is more than slightly modified - in fact it's one of the fastest around.

50

51

52

53

54

55

56

57

54. Midget rear lights are just to help you to see what it's supposed to be – not much else is recognisable!

55. Beneath the skin, even more differences are on show. There is coil spring rear suspension and look at the rose-jointed axle links.

56. At the front end, grille, lamps and badging help to identify the 'Spridget' base of this lightweight and entirely rebodied car.

57. Front suspension is based on the standard layout - which is some indication of what a good system it is - but those racing slicks give the game away

58

59

60

61

62

63

58. When B.L. first shoe-horned a Triumph 1500 engine into a Midget engine bay, they experimented with S.U. carburettors. Note the amazingly long top hose retained on production cars. Wherever does it go? (Photo: courtesy B.L. Heritage).

59. The car that the 1500 engine was fitted to, seen here in rather elegant surroundings. Raised ride height, huge rubber bumpers and as-you-were rear wheel arches characterised the car.

60. The rubber bumpers in fact concealed an awful lot

of protective steel work behind them. The idea was to make the Midget shell strong enough to get past the extremely stringent US crash damage testing regulations.

61. The US specification Midget was fitted with a number of other modifications including side-marker lamps. A pre-war Midget poses uncomfortably in the background of this publicity shot. (Photo: courtesy B.L. Heritage).

62. Abingdon production, seen here in full swing, is,

alas, no more. The factory was destroyed by B.L. in 1982 and the site is now an industrial estate. In the forground of this picture is a UK specification car while in the background, wire-wheeled US specification cars receive finishing touches.

63. This car was fitted with M.G. instruments but later versions were more 'Triumphised' being fitted with Triumph instruments. The Morris Marina type gearbox gave synchro on first (at last!) but rather unsuitable ratios.

64. The end for the Midget came in November 1979 when the last car was built. How ironic that when the Midget's ancestor, the MkI Sprite was introduced, it was to fill an obvious gap in the market; and when the Midget went it left just the same huge and obvious gap in the market.

65. Mark Smith, the car's proud owner shows off the condition award he won in the first concours for which he entered the car, at an M.G. Owners' Club mini-national meeting.

66. Mark's car's engine bay looks cleaner than most people would think possible. As well as the chroming and customising (not to everyone's taste!), Mark puts in regular hours polishing and cleaning his car and the engine bay in particular.

67. Viewed from the other side it is clear that a dedicated approach and an engine free of oil leaks is essential to maintain this sort of standard.

68. Mark has had the boot nicely carpeted and a very useful cover fits snugly over the spare wheel. Note the boot light and automatic boot stay that were both fitted as standard to the 1500.

69. The passenger door was fitted with the same type of door mirror as the driver's door. Previously it had been optional.

C1

C2

C3

C1. Following the Frogeye was a difficult act. BMC tackled it by building an entirely new bodyshell on the old car's floorplan and mechanical components. This is the Austin-Healey Sprite MkII. The Midget MkI came with trim, chrome and grille differences.

C2. Note the half boot handle on this early Sprite MkII pictured at a Healey club meeting.

C3. At the rear end, wheel arches were made much squarer than the Frogeye's while quickly detachable wire wheels became an attractive option.

C4. Front end styling changes were carried out by Healey themselves. From this angle, the front wing line is highly reminiscent of the "Big" Healeys. Note the pronounced kick-up of the sill - a surviving feature from the Frogeye.

C5. M.G. grilles wore vertical bars which somehow made the cars appear more distinguished than the Austins' cheesegrater grilles.

C4

C5

C6. All-in-all the later Healeys and the new Midgets achieved a harmonious balance of line which belied the fact that the front and rear halves of the car were styled in two different places.

C7. Healeys and Midgets look particularly attractive with the hood down. When fitted with the later style folding top, taking the hood down is a very rapid operation.

C6

C7

C8

C9

C8 & C9. Later cars were taken over by a fit of B.L. corporateness which similarly afflicted MGBs. In contrast to the earlier cars, grilles became black, recessed and adorned with a chrome strip; bumpers were lighter and featured rubber inserts in the over-riders. Thinner front bumpers meant that sidelight positions had to be lowered slightly; a point worth watching on earlier cars which have been restored, since earlier type wings are now unavailable. By now of course, the Sprite had gone for good.

C10. The later 1275cc Midgets came with black painted sills. Note too the half bumpers. Although non-standard, roll-over bars are a popular fitting combining safety with a real macho image ("my car goes so fast that..."). Some models of bar, designed specifically for racing, do not make allowances for the hood and none allow for the tonneau - a point worth bearing in mind when buying.

C10

C11

C12

C11 & C12. Hood-down means that the tonneau comes into its own in Britain, the land of expected unexpected showers. Cars supplied with optional headrests were supplied with a tonneau to suit. Rounded rear wheel arches were restored to the rear end of the later 1275 Midgets and went some way to removing the look of squatness and heaviness which afflicted earlier cars. Neither chrome Rostyle wheels nor chrome cover sills were ever standard items, but they are typical of the treats which proud Sprite and Midget owners give their cars.

C13

C14

WBW 993M

UOC 654H

ANP 362H

C15

C13 & C14. Pre and post-facelift models have distinctive differences in rear-end styling. Not only is the half bumper of the later model lighter in style but it is also positioned higher to give a more harmonious appearance.

C15. A Sprite and two Midgets. Despite the differences in the age and styling of these cars, they all share the same floorpan and the A-series engine

C16

C17

C18

C16. The use of heavy front bumpers on the 1500 Midgets completely transformed the appearance of the front end of the car. The car's suspension was also jacked-up which meant that handling deteriorated, although most commentators agreed that the deterioration was less than that suffered by the similarly ill-treated MGB. A positive side-effect of the jacking-up process was that greater spring travel was gained giving a softer, less old-fashioned ride.

C17. Rear bumpers were equally massive and meant that reversing light positions had to be raised and number plates lowered. The rubber on show covers a lot of heavy steel beneath. The old-style rear wheel arches were reinstated. Some say that it was because the round arches lacked the required strength in rear end crash simulation tests, while others claim that the round arches looked just plain silly when jacked-up above the rear wheels.

C18. Compared with earlier models, particularly the austerity of the original Frogeye, the 'rubber-bumper' 1500cc Midgets were downright luxurious. By this time most of the instruments of the Midget and many major components were common to other B.L. cars.

C19

C19. James Thacker seen in his ModSports Midget in which he is highly competitive. He has progressed from a co-owned ProdSports Midget, through a rapid ex-Alec Poole Frogeye to his present tailor-made car. He is seen here in a Midget race at Donington in June 1981.

C20. This rather unusual car is a WSM Sprite with very distinctive bodywork. It is seen here lapping Silverstone. (Photo: courtesy Chris Harvey)

C20